Praise for *Aging and Loving: Christian Faith and Sexuality in Later Life*

"In search of a realistic ethic of sexuality and relationship that honors the logistical complexity of our senior years, Jim Childs challenges us to think off-script without departing from our Christian vocation to love and be loved. In the process, he gathers LGBTQ and straight Christians under one gracious roof, honoring marriage while finding common ground among all loving relationships."

—Cristina L.H. Traina, Avery Cardinal Dulles Chair of Catholic Theology, Fordham University

"Lutheran ethicist Jim Childs here offers a theologically rich, pastorally sensitive, morally serious, and always deeply dignified treatment of Christian sexual ethics for senior adults. Social changes in recent decades have dramatically reshaped the landscape within which senior adults navigate their sexual choices. The most thoughtful moral analysis is required especially as Christian seniors, and those who accompany them and care for them, seek to discern the way forward. This book could become the indispensable resource for the next stage of that conversation."

—Rev. Dr. David P. Gushee, distinguished university professor of Christian ethics, Mercer University; director, Center for Theology & Public Life, Mercer University; and former president, American Academy of Religion & Society of Christian Ethics

"*Aging and Loving* addresses matters we often ignore, avoid, or talk about clumsily—growing old and sex. Jim Childs names our failings and illuminates the truth with insight, grace, and compassion. He charts a faithful, ethical path that reframes our vision of what the autumn of life can be when we live with the joy and love that are central to the anticipation of God's coming reign. He does so with the discipline of a scholar and the grace, eloquence, and care of a pastor. This is an essential book for all who age and all who care for the aging."

—Timothy V. Olson, lead pastor, Holy Trinity Lutheran Church (ELCA)

"With engaging personal commentary, insightful observations, and his trademark depth of ethical and theological wisdom, Dr. James Childs has given us a book that thwarts ageism. I found myself casting aside myths and biases, and following Dr. Childs into an exploration of the fullness of God-given sexuality that turns out to be relevant not only for older adults, but for all ages and orientations."

—Margaret Payne, former bishop, New England Synod of the ELCA, and chair of the ELCA Task Force on Human Sexuality

AGING *and* LOVING

AGING *and* LOVING

CHRISTIAN FAITH AND SEXUALITY IN LATER LIFE

JAMES M. CHILDS JR.

FORTRESS PRESS
MINNEAPOLIS

AGING AND LOVING
Christian Faith and Sexuality in Later Life

Print ISBN: 978-1-5064-6641-5
eBook ISBN: 978-1-5064-6642-2

Cover design: Marti Naughton (sMart desigN)
Cover images: Hourglass © Anigoweb | Dreamstime.com
Background © Myszka50 | Dreamstime.com

Contents

Part Three
MAPPING THE WAY OF CHRISTIAN LOVE

Preface

I begin with a little personal history and how events in that history led to the writing of this book. While I took my turn teaching a course in human sexuality every three years for a couple of decades or more, this had not been my primary field of study in theology and ethics. During my college and university teaching years, I certainly did have units on sexual ethics in introductory courses. I published a good deal, especially after coming to Trinity Lutheran Seminary, now at Capital University, but for some reason, nothing in the area of sexuality.

I often think with some amusement that this lack of publication on the topic of sexuality was probably an asset when the Evangelical Lutheran Church in America (ELCA) called me to direct the church-wide study on the church and homosexuality. At the time, 2002, this was a very contentious issue, so not having published on the subject meant I had a chance to be regarded as fair and as unbiased as a normal mortal can be. That didn't stop opponents of the study from trying to cast doubt on my integrity, but at least they couldn't quote something I'd written as damning evidence!

I accepted the church's call to be the director of sexuality studies for the study entitled *Journey Together Faithfully: The Church and Homosexuality.*[1] I remained in that position on loan from the seminary from February 2002 through September 2005, at which point my work and that of our task force was complete. I stayed on for the next phase as an advisory member when the newly constituted task force took up the crafting of a social statement (*Human Sexuality: Gift and Trust*[2]) to deal with all facets of sexuality. They were also tasked to make recommendations on whether the church could welcome persons in committed same-sex unions into its ministries. In 2009, the ELCA voted to admit qualified persons in committed same-sex unions into the ordained, commissioned, and consecrated ministries of the church. I like to think that our study that began in 2002 laid the groundwork for this breakthrough.

Those years of work for the church on matters of sexuality thrust me deeply into the subject matter. When my tenure was complete and I was free to express my own position, I presented a paper at the Society of Christian Ethics that was subsequently published in the *Journal of the Society of Christian Ethics* entitled "Eschatology, Anthropology, and Sexuality: Helmut Thielicke and the Orders of Creation Revisited."[3] It is a theological challenge to the orders-of-creation argument against same-sex unions, a challenge that affirms the theological validity of such unions. Elements of that paper appear in chapter 5 of this book, and the learnings from years in sexuality studies for the church are reflected throughout.

The next opportunity to delve into questions of faith and sexuality came as a result of my membership on the editorial board of *Dialog: A Journal of Theology*. At our annual meeting, we discuss possible topics for upcoming issues. It was decided that we would publish an issue on aging. It occurred to me right away that for all that had been published in recent years on sexuality and in my own work and teaching on the subject, I could think of nothing on sexuality in later life from the vantage point of the Christian faith. I volunteered to write on that aspect of aging. The result was the publication of "Aging and Sexuality" in *Dialog*, December 2019.[4] The process of researching for this article led me to the conviction that there was much more that needed to be said. Thus the article became the springboard for the book. I am grateful to the guest editor of that issue of *Dialog*, Dr. Ernest Simmons, and to the editor of *Dialog*, Dr. Kristin Largen, for affording me the opportunity to write on the subject and approving it for publication. My involvement with this journal has always been a most rewarding experience.

I have others to thank as well. First of all, I want to thank Scott Tunseth, the editor of this project at Fortress Press, for his support of its publication and helpful conversation during the process. A special word of gratitude goes to my friend and colleague Dr. Linda Mercadante, who read the draft of the manuscript and offered insightful comments. Roland Hornbostel, Katy Allen, Susan Wallace, Peter van Runkle, Beth Long-Higgins, Tim R.

Johnston, and Jane Fleischman kindly provided consultation and direction to resources for various aspects of the narrative.

I hope that this book will be helpful to the various professionals who minister to the aged, to their families, and to the aging and aged themselves. The focus is on people sixty-five years old and older. This is the age group whose sexuality is most vulnerable to being dismissed by those around them. It is also the age group that experiences new challenges to their sexual lives as age brings physical and sometimes psychological changes as well as changes in living circumstances.

To be human is to be sexual. To undermine or fail to appreciate that fact in older age and to regard the diminishments of aging as the end of sexuality and therefore the dissipation of fully meaningful life are critical dimensions of ageism that are, like other "isms," hurtful. My goal in this book is twofold: to shed light on the realities of sexuality in later life and the choices older adults face and to provide a theological account that affirms their sexuality as integral to their humanity and vocation in later life. By doing so, I hope to curb the paternalistic attitudes of ageism that are so harmful to the aged, the aging, and their families. This is essential in equipping those who care for them and minister to them. To this end, the purpose is to enable professionals who minister to the aged and all those related to the aged to have a deeper respect for their sexuality—and thus their dignity—and to provide an ethical account of Christian love that liberates as it engages the special issues of sexuality in later life.

Part One

Confronting Perception and Reality

Chapter One

ATTITUDES TOWARD AGING AND SEXUALITY

> Listen to your father who begot you, and do not despise your mother when she is old.
>
> —Proverbs 23:22

The following excerpts from the United Nations' 1999 report of the International Year of Older Persons provide points of reference for the challenges that are before us: a burgeoning and longer-lived population of older adults and the need to overcome lingering prejudices about old age and affirm the dignity and possibilities of later life:

> Old age is a new frontier. In the second half of the twentieth century, twenty years have been added to the average life-expectancy worldwide. As pioneers of this life-extension, today's elders are re-writing the scripts for late-life, exploring new ways of being, becoming, and doing in the high age.[1]

> A society for all ages is one that does not caricature older persons as patients and pensioners. Instead, it sees them as both agents and beneficiaries of development. It honours traditional elders in their leadership and consultative roles in communities throughout the world.[2]

Our particular concerns with aging and sexuality find their place within this larger context of aging in the twenty-first century. The goal of this book is to uphold the dignity of the aged and enable a deeper understanding and respect for their sexuality while providing a theological and ethical account of Christian love that liberates and motivates as it engages the special issues of sexuality in later life.

Old Age: Geezers, Codgers, and Dotty Old Grannies?

In a recent adult class on aging in a local congregation, I asked the members of the class to voice what comes to their minds when they think about aging or being old. Here are some of the ideas they came up with:

- *Retirement:* For those still fit and having the wherewithal, this means opportunities for new and rewarding experiences. It may also mean the loss of meaningful work and the self-worth invested in it as well as feeling the loss of belonging to a workplace family.
- *Loss:* Older age often means the loss of friends, vigor, and perhaps a spouse, and with such losses comes the prospect of *loneliness*, compounded for some by being homebound or in a nursing home.
- *Physical changes and health issues:* Health generally diminishes; maybe memory loss or even senility intrude into one's life.
- *Devalued and dependent:* Feeling devalued as one becomes more and more dependent on the care of others is a perceived fear in older age.
- *Regrets:* As time for new beginnings and the healing of old wounds slips away, regrets may plague the memories of older adults.
- *Stereotypes:* The aged are often characterized as feeble, frail, crabby, set in their ways, and needy.
- *Wisdom:* The accumulated experiences of many years and the lessons learned can be the source of wisdom that older folks have to pass on. (For my own part, I suspect some of that wisdom, forged by hard experience, is to be a bit less judgmental of others and more attuned to the ambiguities of life. This is a thought to which I shall return later.)

Clearly, most of the thoughts expressed reflect negative perceptions of what old age is all about. However, it was also clear from the conversation that while the class was identifying very real concerns that come with advanced age, they themselves held a more positive attitude toward aging and the aged and toward the prospects for their quality of life. Their more positive attitudes toward older folks can be put down to their faith-based sense of respect and kindness toward people of all ages. Their more positive outlook on quality of life in old age may be put down to their sense that later life has gotten better for many; one may remain active and healthy much longer than in past generations. In any case, the comments arising from this small, unrehearsed, albeit rather demographically homogeneous sample reflect the range of thinking about old age in our society.

Though not spoken of in these terms, the more positive thoughts from the class about aging reflect the prospects of life in what gerontologists have come to call the "third age." In developed countries, the third age—usually thought of as beginning with retirement, perhaps at age sixty-five—is marked by new opportunities and an active, still-healthy life. The "fourth age" is marked by the onset of diminished physical and mental capacities and greater dependence. Some have arbitrarily set age eighty or eighty-five as the beginning of the fourth age.[3] The negative comments from the class are the sorts of impressions usually associated with the fourth age.

The conditions identified with the third and fourth ages are not set in stone, however, since differences in life situations may mean that some people experience the characteristics of the fourth age earlier in life, while others may retain the vigor of the third age longer than one normally expects. In individual cases, variables such as genetic inheritance, poverty, lifestyle, and illness or disability may affect the process of aging in various ways not characteristic of other older adults. Recent studies have also shown a positive connection between religious faith, including church attendance, and psychological well-being, positive health status, and life satisfaction.[4]

The demarcation of aging into third and fourth ages is a useful device for studies of gerontology and helps focus our understanding of aging. Similarly, the studies we will look at later regarding the sexuality of older adults will also provide a greater understanding of later life. However, in the final analysis, we are always engaged personally or relationally at the individual level, with all its physical, emotional, ethical, and religious particularities.

Despite the active and independent lifestyles of many older adults in our society, stereotypes and perceptions like some that were voiced in our class discussion linger in our culture. Researcher Jeanette C. Takamura believes that our preoccupation with youth may contribute to the negative images of the elderly—fuddy-duddy geezers who are devalued and disrespected as irrelevant, odd, impotent, and past their prime. She lists six popular myths of aging that illustrate simplistic and distorted views of old people: (1) to be old is to be sick, (2) you can't teach an old dog new tricks, (3) the horse is out of the barn, (4) the secret to successful aging is to choose your parents wisely, (5) the light may be on but the voltage is low, and (6) the elderly don't pull their own weight.[5] Some of these are well-worn clichés and may even spark a note of amusement in some cases, but they are myths or stereotypes nonetheless.

Myths and stereotypes are the stuff of ageism. Psychologist Robert Youdin speaks of three types of ageism. *Personal* ageism is the practice of younger people stigmatizing older adults as incompetent or incapable of functioning properly. *Institutional* ageism occurs when institutions enact policies or allow practices that discriminate against the aged. A distressing example of this kind of ageism happens in some nursing homes when residents are abused verbally, physically, or sexually because they complain about the lack of service or are regarded with disdain because of their dementia. *Intentional* ageism, similar to institutional ageism, refers to deliberate measures that discriminate against older adults, as in employment opportunities or workplace advancement.[6] According to Keith C. Meador and Shaun C. Henson, "Ageism is the gerontological equivalent to racial prejudice or sexism, where in this case 'ageism' or unfair generalizations about any who are old are routinely made. Discrimination in this regard takes place in both subtle and overt ways. 'All elderly people are forgetful,' 'all elderly people are ill tempered,' 'all elderly people suffer from depression,' 'mental impairment is endemic to aging,' 'most elderly people have no interest in, and cannot enjoy sex,' are several sweeping statements."[7]

Not all would agree that ageism is the equivalent of racial prejudice, but ageist generalizations of this kind are distortions that cause harm to those being characterized in these ways. Simply put, they are hurtful. Ageist attitudes and stereotypes develop early in life, just as racism and sexism often do. Surprisingly, some studies show that when ageism is sustained in a person's attitude, it adversely affects the quality of later life and health, whereas a positive attitude toward aging has a positive effect on future health.[8] Furthermore, when older folks internalize the stereotypes to which they are submitted, that behavior is reinforced, like a self-fulfilling prophecy. This is one of the insidious effects of stereotypes.[9]

No One Wants to Think of Their Elderly Parents or Grandparents Having Sex, Do They?

The sweeping generalizations and stereotypes concerning the aged feel even more negative when it comes to matters of sexuality in later life. For many, old age and sexuality don't go together. When you reach age sixty-five, the start of the third age, and certainly when you enter the fourth age, it is not unusual for people to think that the days of sexual activity are over. After all, one's physical appearance, vitality, and sexual capacities are in decline. The elderly are thought of by many as virtually asexual. Frits de Lange quotes Simone de Beauvoir's statement, which he considers an accurate rendering of a long history of aversion to aging in Western classical traditions as well as in Eastern cultures: "If old people show the same desires, the same feelings and same requirements as the young, the world looks upon them with disgust: in them love and jealousy seem revolting and absurd, sexuality repulsive and violence ludicrous."[10]

De Beauvoir's assessment reflects the fact that negative opinions concerning old age in general lay the foundation for negative attitudes toward old-age sexuality in particular. Since sex is related to mental maturity in the popular mind, the "desexualization" of older people is a function of the "infantilization" of older people—the tendency to treat them like children.[11] Moreover, "if having sexual intercourse is one of the key factors in determining whether you are perceived as 'sexual' or not, then evidence that the rates of sexual intercourse decline into later life obviously contribute to the characterization of old age as asexual."[12]

While all people would not caricature the elderly in unflattering terms, the fact is that older people live their lives in a context where the disparagement of age in general and aging and sexuality in particular remain salient factors. Perhaps disparaging judgments are not always blatant but simply reinforced by silence—a refusal to acknowledge the reality of a sexual life in old age or even to discuss the matter. Certainly, in our youth culture, in which sexuality is the province of the young and beautiful, the sexuality of older folks is de facto marginalized.

The media in advertising, television programming, and film make this youth-and-beauty bias clear, with few exceptions. Advertisements featuring young, attractive men and women are the norm. As everyone knows, sex sells, and "sex" in this case is a function of youthful beauty. Vigorous young women sell fitness equipment, shoes, and clothing. Older women are besieged by ads featuring products designed to combat the wrinkles and creping that come with age. The message is clear, and it appeals to the anxiety that social pressure creates as aging progresses. Not all women are susceptible to these approaches, but sales figures suggest that many are.

Films and cable TV offerings, which now commonly include graphic nudity and sexual activity, do not portray older people in such explicit encounters. As one respected study has observed, "Portrayals of sexual older people in film are mostly limited to affectionate or romanticized relationships of the 'well preserved,' with sex not actually shown but only hinted at."[13]

My attention was drawn recently to the song "Keep Young and Beautiful," which appears in the televised revival of the musical *42nd Street*. First performed in 1933 in *Roman Scandals*, the song was not in the original 1980 production of *42nd Street*. Considering our present climate of strong opposition to sexist sentiments, its inclusion in this contemporary offering was a surprise. Here is a portion of the lyrics:

> *Keep young and beautiful*
> *It's your duty to be beautiful*
> *Keep young and beautiful*
> *If you want to be loved.*[14]

Some may well be offended by the song, since it reflects unsavory male attitudes toward women. Others may toss it off as simply historical, suited to the time frame of the play, no big deal. Nonetheless, the lyrics do express a persistent legacy of equating being beautiful with being loved. In fact, I suspect most people still believe it's true that staying beautiful is important, if not essential, to having a good love life.

Beyond my suspicion in this regard, researchers have confirmed what, for many, is obvious—namely, that women, more than men, do live under this pressure to stay beautiful in order to be loved. There is a socially constructed ideal of what is beautiful and sexy, and "the extent to which women can conform to this ideal becomes a marker of their sexuality—the shape of a woman's body, the size of her breasts, and the color of her hair, are features commonly used to assess her value as a sexual being."[15] This is a heavy demand at any age and a source of great anxiety and emotional pain for many younger women. For older women, as age takes its inevitable toll on the body, the expectation of enduring beauty becomes increasingly difficult if measured by the standards of society.

As the study also indicated, older men may fare better in terms of the demand for physical beauty as a condition of sexual attractiveness. However, this is not true in every case. Ron Long, writing from the perspective of a gay male, speaks of how youthful male beauty is associated with values of goodness, and "beauty of body is a metaphor for beauty of the soul."[16] He continues, "Gay material culture is replete with images of beautiful men—and images of beautiful men having sex. It seems to me that photography and porn are the media through which gay men experience the 'wholly beautiful.' Porn represents ideal 'togetherness'—while the beautiful man represents ideal 'beingness.' And together they represent the perfection of existence."[17]

This cultural reality places heavy burdens on the self-esteem of aging gay men whose physical attributes and sexual prowess are fading. Even Christian theologians, Long observes, thought that at the resurrection, we would all have thirty-year-old bodies, the age thought to be the prime of our attractiveness. Thus in this account, he contends, beauty is defined by *youthful* beauty for all eternity.

After a wide-ranging philosophical and theological argument, Long concludes that aging provides "a challenge to develop the metaphoric depths of character that are suggested by those very features of our bodily life that time erodes."[18] In other words, the innate goodness associated with the physical beauty of youth in gay culture may in fact be better attained by the older man whose beauty has faded but whose grasp of life has increased. The analogy he gives is about walking: "Walking is really a balancing act in motion. But while the young man walks easily, he is not yet disciplined in how to balance the claims that life may make upon him. We indulge him his wild oats as he seeks to discover himself. The corresponding virtue in the mature man is the 'balancing' of the affairs of his life and day."[19]

Though the above is an article about gay life and aging with its own particular realities, its message of finding self-worth and personal value when aging in the context of a youth culture can speak to all people. It is a positive note that will find expression in various ways as our narrative proceeds. Meanwhile, we can't ignore the fact that older people can easily internalize feelings of sexual inferiority in our culture of youth and beauty.

The Shame Factor

Jennifer Hillman, a psychologist, writes of a seventy-six-year-old woman named Jayne who had been divorced for twenty-five years. There was a man who showed interest in dating and even taking her on a cruise. Though she said she couldn't handle a cruise due to the increasing immobility caused by her arthritis, she also said she couldn't go on a cruise with that man anyway. Despite the fact that her thoughts about this man were uniformly positive, she felt it was wrong for her to be dating and getting involved with a man at her age. When asked why, she responded, "What kind of example would I be setting for the children at church? Old women don't prance around holding hands or kissing somebody much less. I don't know what I'm thinking about!"[20] Hillman goes on to recount how therapeutic intervention helped liberate Jayne from the inhibitions of her religious and social background and enabled her to have a happy relationship, even a sexual relationship, with this man. However, not all people like Jayne find their way past the negative attitudes about sexuality and aging that are imposed upon them.

Contemporary studies have found that people see sex among older adults as nonexistent, shameful, disgusting, and even laughable. As with other ageist stereotypes like those we have reviewed earlier in the chapter, when internalized by older people, the result is potentially harmful. In this case, living with these perceptions can have a repressive effect on older adults who may fear that their sexual feelings and desires are unacceptable in light of these perceived social norms. Living under the spell of such fears "can in turn cause 'irrational prohibitive feelings' about aging sexuality and negatively affect sexual experiences and relationships."[21]

The implied censure of desultory and even derisive stereotypes of old-age sexuality may be a source of shame when older adults struggle with sexual desire. As the study suggests, the implied censure of stereotypical stigmata is easily blended with a legacy of strict and prohibitive sexual ethics. Older adults grew up under the sway of that legacy. Despite recent developments of more permissive attitudes, traditional norms of sexual conduct can remain a part of their consciousness and conscience, even among the older of the supposedly more liberated "baby boomers." This burden of sexual morality can be particularly challenging to single older adults, especially those who hold to a religious faith with strict moral codes concerning sexual conduct.

We do well, then, to remind ourselves of our heritage of sexual morality and the degree to which it has had a somewhat inhibiting effect on matters of human sexuality. For Christians, the seeds of reserve and ambivalence about sexual desire and activity are already present in the New Testament, specifically chapter 7 of Paul's first letter to the Corinthians. In verse 1, we read, "It is well for a man not to touch a woman" (1 Corinthians 7:1). This appears to set the table for a number of interpretations that follow. First of all, it intimates that women are by nature a dangerous source of sexual temptation. This is a view that also finds expression in a tradition of the female temptress grounded in the story of temptation and fall in the garden of Eden (Genesis 3) and carried forward through the ages. It is hard to overestimate the damage done to women by this mode of thought. It also sexualizes all male-female encounters, which de facto confirms the need for highly restrictive rules governing those relationships. Second, though celibacy is acknowledged as a gift that not all have, it is to be preferred

(1 Corinthians 7:7, 26, 32, 38). Third, marriage appears primarily as a curb against lustful passions and for those who lack self-control (1 Corinthians 7:9, 36). All in all, sexuality is morally hazardous territory.

Interpreters have sought to mitigate the disparaging view of women and sexuality reflected in these verses by contending that they are not the final word on what the Bible teaches but part of the cultural scenery of Paul's context. Also cited are Paul's expectation that the eschaton was near and, therefore, his concern that Christians be prepared for it and not caught up in the matters of this age, such as marriage (1 Corinthians 7:29, 31). These are valid considerations for how we finally understand Paul on sexuality. For the present discussion, it is simply the case that the ambivalent view of sexuality implied in Paul's writings has had a lasting impact on Christian sensibilities about sex.

Early Christian theologians, in turn, held to a rather pessimistic view of sexuality. Since the fall, sexual desire was thought to be tainted by sinful desires. However, as part of the good creation, sexual intercourse could be affirmed for the sake of procreation within the framework of marriage. Dominant figures such as Augustine and, centuries later, Thomas Aquinas advanced the procreation principle, which says that sexual activity outside the purposes of procreation in marriage is sinful. This principle endured in Roman Catholic tradition into the twentieth century until it was modified, at first, to say that sexual intercourse without procreational intent could serve the good purpose of spousal union. Finally, it was further modified to allow that both the intent to procreate and the bonding in love of husband and wife were equal goods. Luther and Calvin championed marriage over the mandate of clerical celibacy. Their view of sex in marriage was not dependent on the procreation ethic. Yet they still shared some of that Augustinian pessimism about human sin and its disordered sex drive. Salutary as these developments were for the status of sex in marriage, they still leave a whole range of sexual activity out of bounds and considered shameful.[22]

Fast-forward now to the mid-twentieth century, the time of my youth, the time depicted in television's *Happy Days*. Even though sexual intercourse in marriage had long been liberated from the taint of original sin in principle, many still believed that sexual desires were dangerous and open to lustful and exploitative intentions, even in marriage. Not all sex in marriage was "good" sex. My father had been schooled in that doctrine. True as this may be, it also created a sense for many that sexual initiatives in marriage could be unsettling, and being a sexual partner might end up being more of a duty than a joy.

Boys and men especially, it was thought, were given to selfish, lustful impulses. Girls were in danger of getting a "reputation" if they weren't guarded in their behavior with boys. They could be called a "slut." My mother, in fact, warned me when I began dating that "all a girl has is her reputation," and I had better respect that. Conservative churches sought to protect young people from the dangers of sexual desire by prohibiting dancing, which they reasoned could lead to more intimate forms of physical contact. Meanwhile, boys worried about the ill effects of masturbation that they had been warned about; these were the wages of sin. I guess we assumed at the time that girls didn't do it. If they did, no one spoke of it. Immorality was equated with sexual sins; if you said the word *immoral*, it was assumed that it meant something about sex rather than other immoral behavior such as lying, cheating, or uttering and promoting racist slurs.

In polite society, people did not speak of sexual matters openly. In fact, sex education in my school days was practically nonexistent. Many parents found themselves tongue-tied when it came to talking to their children about sex. Sex was hidden from view like the condoms sold in the drug store, which were not on display as they are today but kept in a drawer behind the counter. They had to be requested, frequently in the hushed tones of an embarrassed customer. Moreover, such a request might even be greeted with questions about one's age and marital status.

Even though many parents didn't speak with their children about sex, they had concerns that outside influences might have a bad effect on their kids' thoughts about sex and what they may lead to. My mother was a member of a PTA committee formed to monitor the sexual content of magazines being sold at the local newsstands. She had a box of this material, which she kept in the attic. As it happened, the door to the attic was in my room. So it was no problem for me to steal up there and read the stuff. Needless to say, those supposedly risqué magazines were nothing in comparison to the material now available in the various media to which people, young and old, have access.

In the churches and in society, sexuality was heterosexuality, and all other expressions of sexual life that fell outside the heteronormativity of the times were severely censured and often persecuted. Sex outside of marriage was clearly a grave sin, and girls or young women who got pregnant out of wedlock were often tragically forced into marriage or sent away, perhaps to an institution, to have the baby out of sight of the community.

Things have changed in the theologies of the church to some degree, and the norms of morality in contemporary society have changed significantly from those of the social milieu in mid-twentieth-century America. An increasingly secularized culture has opened the door to more permissive attitudes toward sexual conduct. At the same time, faith communities try to rethink, yet sustain, fundamental norms of sexual conduct as they respond to the cultural shifts. At this point, we are not ready to consider those changes. I simply want to briefly characterize the moral climate of a time when the consciences of many older adults were being shaped. Not all of the aged, their family members, and their caregivers have embraced the changes that have come. Blend this deposit of traditional and religious norms with imposed negative stereotypes of old-age sex, and you have a recipe for shame—a sense that the sexual desires of your old age are shameful and somehow deeply disordered.

Adrian Thatcher, who has written extensively on theology and sexuality, speaks of the Christian tradition of ambivalence toward sexuality as "Christianity's battle with *eros*."[23] One of the consequences of this battle is the problem of sexual shame, a concept he borrows from Karen McClintock's book *Sexual Shame*.[24] Thatcher likes the definition of shame as "an inner sense of being completely diminished or insufficient as a person."[25]

Shame may be distinguished from guilt. We feel guilty for doing something we realize is wrong. We are sorry, and we feel that this behavior is out of character for us. We may seek forgiveness and pledge to do better. But with shame, there is a sense that, more than having done wrong, we are no longer good, we are wrong at the core—or as McClintock puts it, there is "a growing sense of disgust with oneself."[26] Sexual shame is renewed each time the feelings and desires that prompted it recur.[27]

Of course, people of all ages may feel ashamed of their sexual desires and practices. They know by how their conscience has been shaped that they have done something deeply wrong. Older adults have the additional burden of being shamed by the idea that sexual desires and activities at their age are innately inappropriate and even disgusting, regardless of the morality or immorality of their conduct and desires as judged by conventional norms.

There is another side to shame: shame over one's aging body and/or shame at being unable to be the sexual person you once were. Arthur Krystal shares these sobering thoughts: "Who the hell wants to tear his or her clothes off at seventy-five? Now we dim the lights and fold our slacks and hope we don't look too soft, too wrinkled, too old . . . the loss of pleasure in one's own body, the loss of pleasure in knowing that one's own body pleases others, is a real one."[28] To that we add this from psychologist Sylvan Tomkins: "Old age is the prime occasion of shame . . . because there is both a heightening of the zest for life and a heightening of all the impediments to enjoyment of life to which the aging body is vulnerable."[29]

While many still feel inhibited by traditional strictures, others who grew up with the sexual revolution (1960s–80s) may experience a different cause for shame. This aging cohort may feel shame for no longer being able to perform sexually as they once did and felt they had to in order to ride the wave of sexual liberation. Women who felt freed to be sexually active in ways their mothers would have deemed shameful may now be ashamed of the fact that in old age, they can no longer perform to the expectations of the culture that shaped their sense of sexuality.

For all generations in the older age group, it is not only fading beauty that stands in the way of a more robust sex life. It is also the onset of physical limitations that can make a person feel ashamed of their body and its sexual shortcomings; they feel they have become a lesser person somehow. So they may give in to the attitudes of some in the younger generation who see old-age sex as unseemly. We will speak more about the physical limitations that affect women and men. Meanwhile, it is enough to observe that those physical issues, along with judgmental norms, cultural pressures, and damaging stereotypes, can create a sense of shame among older adults.

THE FEAR FACTOR

According to gerontologist Merryn Gott, "It can be argued that old age is characterized as asexual because of our obsession with the sexual and our deep fear of old age."[30] This is representative of the widespread ageism in our society. With echoes of Ron Long's analysis of sexuality in gay culture, Gott maintains that sexuality represents everything that is "good" in our sexualized society: power, wealth, beauty, and youth. She continues, "Old age by contrast represents all that is feared about being human—dependency on others, economic disenfranchisement, ugliness, sickness, and death."[31]

Fear can create distance. We avoid that which we fear, sometimes for good reason, but often to our detriment and that of those whom we fear. Thus it is not unusual for people to feel uncomfortable with the very old. It is not unusual for people to feel uncomfortable with visiting the sick and the dying.

Fear can also express itself in cruelty. We see that all the time in people's fear of those who are different. It may not be admitted, but their difference is felt as a threat to the well-being of the fearful. Cruel attitudes and actions toward those of other races, ethnicities, and sexual orientations are commonplace. Disdain for those whose sexuality is other than the heteronormative is at base a fear that diverse expressions of sexuality threaten the stability of what many think of as the divine order of creation. During my time directing our church-wide sexuality study, people often expressed their fear that if we were to bless same-sex unions, the meaning of their own marriage and family would be threatened; it could no longer represent God's will for humanity. Likewise, fear of our own aging and with it the loss of sexual desirability and potency, not to mention the shadow of death, can express itself in the dismissal and avoidance of the elderly that is cruel in its own way, however indirect. They are "them," not "us"! This may compound the feelings of loneliness and abandonment that many experience in old age.

If, as Gott maintains, people regard the old as asexual because age summons visions of sickness, dependency, and death, how is it that we make that connection? For Gott, as we have seen, it is because our sexualized culture identifies sexuality with the goods of youth, beauty, and vitality, whereas old age, being none of those things by societal standards, cannot be sexual. This is a highly plausible argument. However, there is, I would suggest, a way to expand on Gott's account from a biblical perspective. The fears described in the face of the realities of aging are all issues of *control*—of our capacity for self-determination in matters that concern us most. The more control slips away, the less we feel like our whole selves.

To pursue this point, I suggest we turn first to the beginning chapters of Genesis. The creation account in Genesis 1 tells us that humanity was created in the image of God and in God's likeness and that God gave humanity the responsibility for the creation as God's representative. From this we discern what the entire biblical witness supports: humanity is created for a special and immediate relationship with God that defines the nature of human existence. The responsibility for the care of the earth that goes with it means that human beings have the freedom to take responsibility for which they are accountable. Freedom and responsibility go together as marks of personhood. The meaning of the image of God in humanity is that we are created for personal communion with God. We are on "speaking terms with God," as theologian George Forell once put it.

Since our very existence is grounded in our relation to God, our being is *dependent* being. Humanity is *image* of God, but not God. This dependent existence is given visual expression by the Hebrew word *tselem*, which is translated as "image" (Genesis 1:26). This is the Hebrew word for a carved image or statue. Kings of the ancient Near East placed their *tselem*, their image, in territories they conquered to give visual expression to their authority. The image was not the king but represented the king. So as image of God, we represent God in the care of the creation; we are dependent and must seek God's will and guidance in that responsibility and in all our relations with one another.

What the story of the fall then tells us in Genesis 3 is that the universal plight of humankind is shaped by our resistance to dependent being. It is a matter of control—to be in charge of your own life without dependence on God. This was the serpent's seductive promise when offering the forbidden fruit: "You will not die; for God knows that when you eat of it your eyes will be opened, and you will be like God, knowing good and evil" (Genesis

3:4–6). In succumbing to the temptation, the story tells us, humanity has stepped away from its life-giving relationship with God; we have shed our "creaturehood" in a desire to control our own destiny.

For many, the vision of old age that evokes fear is one of lost control and the dependency that comes with the diminishing capacities of aging. No amount of time in the gym will forever forestall the onset of aging's effects. Healthy habits represent good stewardship of life but should not be a source of smug self-satisfaction. As sexual beings, the loss of control over our sexual lives that comes with reduced sexual vitality can be an additional fearsome prospect. Lurking in the fear of lost control over life is the often-unspoken realization that humanity's pretense of independent existence has been a grand delusion, with death as the last word.

Viewing later life through this lens of fear results in a distortion that shrinks the worth of the aged. It is ironic, perhaps, that from the standpoint of biblical anthropology, dependency is the source of life and its ultimate hope. I speak, of course, of a dependency on God, who in Christ's redeeming work completes the plan of creation for communion and union with God that knows no end. It is a dependency that is the way of everlasting life. Moreover, the command to love both God and neighbor tells us that we are created and destined for a dependency on one another as well. A brief account of the theology of the Trinity helps make this point.

In the doctrine of the Trinity, we understand the unity of the three persons in the one divine life to be a dynamic relational unity in which the Father, Son, and Spirit remain distinct while yet participating in the very life of one another in the most intimate way imaginable. It is a unity in difference solidified in the bonds of love. Indeed, we can say not only that God is loving, but more than that, God *is* love. This is the essence of the divine life as God has revealed God's self in our history. Created in God's image, we are created in the image of the Trinity for a life of love with God and one another that reflects the same nature of community and unity that is God's life. We are thus mutually dependent on one another, not mainly for services or needs, but existentially for the community that is our birthright in the image of the Triune God.

Certainly, we enjoy our independence, and being dependent on others in old age, as in sickness at any age, can be onerous in itself and more so if we are not well cared for. We cannot minimize this reality. We simply need to recognize that our independence and the freedom of choice that goes with it is, at any age, relative and limited by our finite capacities and the outside forces at work in our lives. We are never completely in control. The life of love for which we are created in the image of the Trinity means giving of ourselves and governing our personal choices for the benefit of the beloved. The desire to be in complete control is the bane of loving, and loving is the nature and destiny of our lives. We will have much more to say about the life of love later, both in the ways we often fail in living it out and in the ways we can live it out. But for the present, what we learn from our existence in the image of the Trinity is that we are made by love and for love. This lasts *forever*. Therefore, in all stages of life, we are lover and beloved. This is true in all relations of life and in and through the expression of our sexuality. There is, from this theological perspective, no basis for dismissing the worth of the old or their sexuality.

VOCATION

We started our project reviewing some of the attitudes that are typical of ageism in general. This is the larger context within which attitudes toward sexuality in later life are located. We then saw how attitudes and perceptions about aging and sexuality are clearly related to attitudes and perceptions about old age in general. Therefore, before we proceed to delve into the multiple aspects of sexuality in later life, it is important, without ignoring the problems of aging, to provide a more positive account of life in old age from the standpoint of our faith. First, a prelude to that conversation.

Coming of Age: The Story of Our Century by Those Who Lived It is one of Studs Terkel's many acclaimed books of oral history.[32] In *Coming of Age*, he records interviews with seventy older Americans from various walks of life with ages ranging from the seventies to the nineties, the youngest at seventy and the oldest at ninety-nine. (Terkel himself lived to ninety-six.) The interviewees share the stories of their experiences and reflect on life as they enter into or already inhabit old age.

Several things need to be said in general as one reads these oral histories. First of all, many, if not most, of the interviewees are still active, working, or engaged in causes. They share a certain indomitable character. Obviously the prevalence of this trait is due to Terkel's process of selection. We cannot generalize about all older adults on the basis of this particular group of people. Though many speak of the typical ailments of advanced age such as arthritis, we don't find in this group anyone who is bedridden, totally dependent, or slipping into senility. That said, the witness to their vitality provides a corrective to the sort of demeaning stereotypes we reviewed at the beginning of this chapter.

The second noteworthy thing about these interviews is the historical memory these older adults possess. This is a historical memory of specific times, circumstances, and places that are important to families and communities and institutions—the multiple personal, familial, and local histories within the larger social history. Finally, the wealth of experience and the learning that has gone with it is of vital importance to the younger generation. For that reason, it is important that we not succumb to ageist assumptions like "The light is still on, but the voltage is low" and fail to be open to what older folks have to share.

A selection drawn from individual interviews gives us further insight into the contributions of these older Americans. David Brower's interview opens the book. He is seventy-nine going on eighty. He is and remains a longtime environmental activist and is cantankerous by his own description. At his age, he observes, one has the freedom to take risks for the cause, whereas younger folks have family and financial obligations that limit their choices. He speaks of all the files and visual images stored in the mind of an eighty- or ninety-year-old that have to be taken out and shared. Certainly, he grants, older people also have to listen to younger folk and not remain stuck in their ways. However, younger people need to pay some attention to the wisdom of age. Were he in an indigenous culture, he observes, at his age he would be an elder who is respected and expected to advise and to be heeded.[33]

Timuel Black, an African American retired schoolteacher of forty years in Chicago, had seen a lot living both through times of blatant discrimination and through the hope of the civil rights movement. He is concerned for the younger generation, whom he thinks has it harder than he did growing up: "My generation's responsibility is to offer them moral support and advice, hoping they'll take it . . . when I was growing up my mother or my father would say, 'we've come this far by faith and we will move further by faith,' the restoration of that faith [for the young] is in the work of the church."[34] His concern for the youth is driven by the faith that shaped his life.

Virginia Bowers is seventy-one and a tutor in Chicago who cares deeply about the children who she knows badly need her help. Her health is poor, she tells Terkel, having had two spinal operations since they last talked. "I try not to let old age bother me," she says. "Sometimes I feel like a hundred, sometimes I feel like a young girl. Some days I don't feel like going. Maybe I've hurt all night long, but I can't stop. These kids are going to be there, and I've got to teach them to *think*."[35]

There are multiple other stories of older people continuing to help younger people in various ways and stories of older people helping other older people. And there are also the important reflections of Sophie Mumford, ninety-four, the widow of Lewis Mumford, the distinguished architecture critic, city planner, culture critic, sociologist, and educator. She relates that she was ignorant and uneducated when she married Lewis. However, through their relationship in marriage, his education and constant intellectual pursuits expanded her horizons over the years of their interesting and engaging conversations on all manner of subjects. She speaks about how she was lonely and at times depressed after Lewis's death, with no one to talk to about the sort of engrossing topics they enjoyed discussing over those many years. She resents the indignities of his illness during his last days and the distressing way it affected his personality.[36]

Sophie adds this sober assessment: "I think this glorification of old age is a great mistake. I resent this whole trend toward increasing the span of life. It used to be three score and ten and you were through. . . . Older people become nonproductive, sad, ill, increasingly self-absorbed because you haven't the energy to go out and do more. Why go on?"[37] For all of that, however, Sophie discovered she was content to go on when certain people started to take an interest in her and communicate with her. Moreover, she considers herself an optimist about the ultimate possibility of being connected with those she loved. Her only concern about death is that it be with dignity. She feels she'd had a good life.[38] From Sophie, we get the gift of a realistic assessment of life's ambiguity—some of the undesirable aspects of old age along with a positive note about life's goodness.

Terkel's interviews and the contributions of the aged that emerge from their narratives remind us that old age and the aged can hardly be defined by the stereotypes so many embrace. Their stories bring me back to the very beginning of this chapter and the conversation on aging we had in our little class. While most of the comments reflected what is perceived as the downside of old age, the idea that older folks have wisdom to share turned the discussion in another direction. We talked about the Christian concept of *vocation* and how it finds expression in later life.

One of the great gifts of the Reformation was the expansion of the theology of *vocation* to include the laity. Prior to this breakthrough, the idea that one had a "calling" from God, a vocation, was restricted to those in holy orders: priests, monks, and nuns. Luther's doctrine of the "priesthood of all believers" provided the basis for this breakthrough. Quoting 1 Peter 2:9, Luther concludes, "Therefore we are all priests, as many of us as are Christians."[39] All have the vocation of being Christ's people in the ministry and mission of the faith. This "ministry of the whole people of God" is lived out in the various occupations and circumstances of life. It may involve the love of one's neighbor in acts of kindness and justice in the workplace. It may be the manner in which parents raise their children in the faith and teach them to pray. It may be sharing the faith with one who needs consolation in the wake of great loss, comfort in the midst of sorrow, or encouragement in the face of failure. It may be one's activism on behalf of the poor and the hungry after the manner of Jesus himself. It may be a teacher who, out of love for the children in her care, uses her own resources to supplement the inadequate supplies the school provides and gives extra time to help the weaker students. In these and many other ways, faith active in love becomes an expression of Christian vocation.

We have come to understand that in baptism, we are ordained to this ministry of the whole people of God. The baptismal liturgy addresses the one to be baptized as "called by the Holy Spirit." The newly baptized are then welcomed: "We welcome you into the body of Christ and into the *mission we share*: join us in giving thanks and praise to God and *bearing God's creative and redeeming word to all the world*." In the service of Affirmation of Baptism, often used at the service of Confirmation, those affirming their baptism are asked, "Do you intend to continue in the covenant God made with you in holy baptism . . . to *proclaim the good news of God in Christ through word and deed*, to serve all people, following the example of Jesus, and to *strive for justice and peace in all the earth*?"[40]

Baptism is for life. We are never not ordained to our vocation's witnesses to the faith in word and deed. There is no retirement from the ministry of the baptized. Many hold to the idea that older people are of less worth because their productivity has diminished by popular standards. From the standpoint of our God-given vocation, that idea is supplanted by the truth of a lifelong calling that defines our identity, purpose, and worth at every age. Terkel was not interested in baptismal vocation, but his interviewees illustrated the sorts of contributions that continue into old age. It did not take the class long to provide their own inspiring accounts of the ways older friends and family members have contributed to family and society. Connecting these gifts to the ministry of the baptized was not hard to do. I think of my father, who gave up his dream of singing with a championship barbershop quartet in order to care for my mother in her fragile health. His self-giving, unassuming, and loving embrace of all his family kept us together at times of tense relationships. Did he have a theology of vocation? No. Did he get up each morning pledging to love as Jesus taught us? I seriously doubt it. But was his unqualified love for us all a true ministry? It certainly was! Even in his last days, when he became more and more dependent on us and on professional care, he never became bitter. So many gifts!

Grandparents often become the joy of their grandchildren, and many take care of them when they have lost their parents or their parents have lost their way. And who has not gone to visit and bring comfort to someone seriously ill or dying and come away saying they received the greater blessing from the witness of that person's faith and the beauty of their serenity? The Christian calling is for life. So as we move further into the discussion of sexuality in later life, we take from these last remarks two things: The stereotypes of old age that devalue older people are not just hurtful; they are wrong. Thus we enter our thoughts on sexuality with that conclusion in mind. Second, from the standpoint of the Christian faith, life at all ages is not only sacred as created in the divine image but also endowed with a gospel vocation that permeates all of life. Our sexual lives are also a venue for that calling.

Further Thoughts

I have absolutely no intention of lumping together the situations of the elderly with situations of persons with physical disabilities. That would be inappropriate. Nonetheless, despite many distinctions that could be drawn between the two populations and the diverse conditions that exist within each, they are both done a similar disservice when it comes to people's attitudes toward their sexuality. Randi S. Chance, a clinical psychologist with a specialty in physical disability, has written compassionately and helpfully as a Christian about the stereotypes that afflict the disabled with respect to their sexuality. She observes that persons with physical disabilities are often thought of as lacking the capacity for normal, satisfying sexual relations. They are frequently seen as asexual, without the same needs and desires for romance and intimacy as folks without disabilities.

As we have seen concerning the damage done by similar stereotypes about older people, stereotypes adversely affect not only the persons themselves but the attitudes and beliefs of the family members and professionals attending to their needs. In the face of this injustice, Chance gives an extensive and enlightening account of the real possibility for love and intimacy among people with disabilities. She affirms their sexuality in no uncertain terms. Her first goal is "to diminish stereotypes in the Christian community in general about the supposed asexuality of people with disabilities and to increase the likelihood that they would be perceived by others as complete well-rounded human beings, with the same needs, desires, and capacities for romantic and sexual relationships as everyone else." Her second objective is to enlighten professionals who work with persons with disabilities.[41] The fact that persons with physical disabilities suffer much the same sort of stereotyping regarding sexuality as do the elderly alerts us to the narrow focus of our society's attitude regarding an understanding of sexuality.

Chapter Two

Sexuality in Older Age

A Reality Check

Let us cherish and love old age, for it is full of pleasure if we know how to use it.

—Seneca, *Letters from a Stoic*

Transition: On *Cloud 9*

In sharp contrast to the various media's tradition of relating sexuality almost exclusively to the young and the beautiful, we have the German film *Cloud 9* (2008), directed by Andreas Dresen. The film tells the story of an adulterous love affair between Inge, sixty-seven, and Karl, in his midseventies. Inge has been married for several decades to Werner, a quiet man whose hobbies are riding trains and listening to recordings of trains. Inge is a seamstress and has just finished alterations on a pair of pants for Karl. She comes to his house to deliver them. They are immediately attracted to one another, and a passionate love scene ensues, with all the explicit nudity you might expect in a Hollywood movie, rated R for "strong sexual content" and "graphic nudity." There is no effort to gloss over the naked reality of their older bodies, with all the marks of age one would expect to see. We are being told that sex between older adults with older bodies is alive and strong.

Inge still has a physical connection to her husband, so the film also has a love scene between Inge and Werner, which Inge initiates. The more passionate lovemaking is that which we see with Karl. Inge is a sexually alive older woman, whom we also see pleasuring herself in the bathtub. Karl, though older, is equally robust in his desires.

In Inge and Karl, we see the depiction of a vital sexuality in older age that goes against the grain of common assumptions that later life is asexual. This message is delivered in the contrast between Werner and Karl. Werner, who likes to see the world on train rides, is "old" in comparison to Karl, who is an active cyclist and loves outdoor activities. Werner typifies the stereotype of old age. I am also struck by the contrast between the sexually involved Inge in her relations with Karl and the recurrent scenes of her singing in a choir of "old ladies," projecting the sort of image people often have of older women who have settled into activities that are appropriate for their age.

The film also voices typical attitudes even as it moves past them. Inge wonders while lying in bed with Karl if she is "not too old for [this] sort of thing." Then after she confesses her infidelity to Werner, despite her daughter's advice not to, Werner chastises her, "Aren't you ashamed of yourself at your age?"

The end is tragic. Inge moves in with Karl, and an inconsolable Werner commits suicide, perhaps by throwing himself in front of a train. The noise of trains passing by as we learn of his death suggests as much. The periodic sound of trains passing throughout the film also suggests the passage of time, which for Inge is a part of her justification of the affair. When Werner tries to convince her to stop this affair, he appeals to the fact that he doesn't have much time left. She responds in kind that she doesn't either. Davide Zordan, whose article on this film drew me into viewing it for this discussion, observes, "Because of this lack of time the self-centeredness of everyone's desire emerges. Karl, too, talks ironically with Inge about the span of time that separates them from the failure of their senses."[1] Self-centeredness in old age can be alive and well at times, as it is at any age. Sexuality can be dangerous in old age at times, as it is at any age. In one of his closing comments on the film, Zordan offers this reflection, which is germane to the work that lies ahead of us in the succeeding chapters:

"How does theology react to this concern with age and sexual desire? Not only classical moral theology, based on the insoluble bond of the unitive and procreative value of sexuality, but also new trends in sexual ethics, are ill-prepared to take up the challenge that this transformation poses. *Elaborating an ethics that ascribes meaning and value to sex, even when every prospect of fertility is excluded (i.e., after menopause) is just the beginning of the work to be done.*"[2]

The "transformation" to which Zordan refers is evident in what the film portrays. It is also evident in the Swedish sociological study he cites concerning the sexual habits of adults over seventy, who are now enjoying sexual activity more than ever. Over a thirty-year span, this has increased significantly: from 52 to 68 percent for married men, from 38 to 52 percent for married women, from 30 to 54 percent for unmarried men, and from 0.8 to 12 percent for unmarried women. Moreover, the data on quality of sex and achievement of orgasm are also significant. The data suggest that the changes are not due so much to the spread of Viagra as to the general improvement in health and quality of life, as well as greater openness to speaking of one's sexual life.[3]

"SEXUALITY"

Before we proceed with further data and stories about sexuality among older adults, we should pause to define what comes under the heading of sexuality. To what do we refer when we speak of "sexuality"? Jennifer Hillman offers the following definition from a clinical perspective:

> Sexuality will be defined here as a *broadly based* term that indicates any combination of sexual behavior, sensual activity, emotional intimacy, or sense of sexual identity. Any individual wish to engage in any of these activities also may be considered an aspect of sexuality. Sexuality may involve sexual activity with the explicit goal of achieving pleasure or climax (e.g., kissing, foreplay, intercourse) . . . or the experience of emotional intimacy within the context of a romantic relationship. Thus, sexuality incorporates a vast number of issues including body image, masturbation,

> love, libido, intercourse, homophobia, relationship satisfaction, marital satisfaction, desires for sexual and sensual experience, and participation in high risk behaviors.[4]

Hillman's extensive definition of what is included in sexuality is reflected in the manifold sexual practices of many older adults: "Older adults engage in a spectrum of sexual and physically intimate behaviors, with masturbation, vaginal intercourse, and foreplay (e.g., kissing, caressing) as the most frequently reported activities. Typical sexual behaviors may shift in older adulthood as the normal aging process affects the physical health and functional capacity of the older adult. In these cases, intimate interactions may focus more on kissing, fondling, cuddling, or the use of assistive devices and medications."[5] Recognizing this broad scope of what is included in sexuality keeps us from making judgments about the reality of sexuality in later life on the basis of a set of criteria that is too narrow. At the same time, we also seek a theological and ethical perspective on the meanings and values we might attach to the experience of our sexuality.

Christian ethicist Margaret Farley has pointed out that the term *sexuality* is relatively new; it has appeared in English dictionaries only since the early nineteenth century. However, despite the dictionaries, she thinks the word's meaning in the abstract is difficult to spell out. Nonetheless, she offers these thoughts: "I take it [sexuality] to include everything that pertains to the sexual—in the sense of sexual desires and loves, feelings, emotions, activities, relationships. As such, sexuality can have physical, psychological, emotional, intellectual, spiritual, personal, and social dimensions . . . private and public meanings, biological and cultural meanings. Sex can refer to genital and non-genital sex, sex with or without desire, sex with or without pleasure."[6]

Farley's comments also alert us to the important fact that the meaning of an action, sexual or otherwise, lies not simply in a description of the action itself; emotional drives and motives, cultural formation, social influences, religious influence, and so on are all part of understanding and evaluating the expressions of our sexuality. Sexuality is "contextual." Her comments suggest an account of sexuality that has to do with the larger meaning of life and questions of values that are at stake in how we live out our sexuality. This is, after all, the concern of her entire book and our concern as well. So inherently theological and ethical questions attach to matters of sexuality after all the dimensions of sexuality are named from Hillman's clinical perspective.

What's Going On?

In the United States, a 2018 survey by the University of Michigan sponsored by the American Association of Retired Persons (AARP) had findings much like those of the Swedish survey that Zordan cited:

> Whether or not they have an active sex life, nearly two-thirds of older adults say they're interested in sex. Men are way more interested than women, however. Half of the 65- to 80-year-old men who were surveyed said they were extremely or very interested in sex, compared with 12 percent of women in that age group. In addition, only 31 percent of the women were sexually active compared with 51 percent of men who reported having sex. The poll did find that 43 percent of women are satisfied with their sex lives, compared with 31 percent of men. . . . More than half of those surveyed also report that sex is important to their quality of life. "Sex and sexual health among older adults doesn't get much attention but is linked closely to quality of life, health and well-being," says Erica Solway, University of Michigan's co-associate director of the poll.
>
> The poll results are based on responses from 1,002 people ages 65 to 80. The margin of error is plus or minus 1 to 3 percentage points among subgroups. Overall, the survey revealed that 40 percent of individuals between ages 65 and 80 are sexually active. Nearly 72 percent of individuals in that age range have a romantic partner and of those, 54 percent are sexually active.[7]

This AARP study echoes the findings of earlier research by the US-based National Social Life, Health, and Aging Project, which showed older adults aged seventy-five to eighty-five having sexual activity two to three times a month in half the cases.[8] These brief summaries of the two reports are sufficient for our present need to simply affirm that the ageist assumptions and stereotypes of asexual older adults that we have already reviewed are not true to reality. Sexual interest and activity continue even among the oldest old and across ethnic populations. On the face of it, one would say this is welcome news and an important corrective to hurtful attitudes. It is. So we can no longer ignore the fact that interest in sex, sexual desires, and sexual activities continue to be a part of life among older adults. Sensitivity to this reality is required of all concerned: families, caregivers, communities, institutions, churches, and the older generation themselves as they relate to one another. However, there is more to be said about the phenomenon of old-age sexuality than a brief summary of statistics can tell us. First, we have a challenge to some of the more enthusiastic reactions.

The "Sexy Oldie"

Recognition of the fact that sexual activity continues into old age has led to a sexualization of older life in both professional and popular literature. Merryn Gott observes that positive messages about the benefits of sex throughout later life are designed to liberate older adults from the persistent myth of asexual old age. However, the result, she argues, has been the creation of a new stereotype, the "sexy oldie." Gott is famous for this idea among gerontologists and health professionals who are advocates of the "positive aging movement," which she is challenging. Five new myths constitute her unfolding of the figment of the sexy oldie and the issues it poses.[9]

Gott's first new myth is that "expressing sexuality (preferably through sexual intercourse) is fundamental to healthy aging." Here she takes to task a variety of articles and studies that assert that sex in later life is good for one's health and well-being and even essential to one's humanity. She maintains that the view that sex is healthy in later life and should be intentionally practiced for healthy aging is a product of expert testimony and certain kinds of media interest rather than the actual experiences and beliefs of older people themselves.[10]

The second new myth is that "sexual intercourse represents the sexual *ideal* for all older people." Thinking about the sex lives of older people in terms of intercourse as the "gold standard," as much of the literature she cites does, downgrades the reality of other forms of sexual intimacy. A number of health factors of old age make intercourse difficult or impossible. The absence of intercourse in a relationship does not mean it is asexual, however. Other forms of intimacy (see Hillman's list of the various practices that we can identify as expressions of our sexuality) are the adjustments people make in later life and are often content with. Cuddling, kissing, and other forms of touch are also part of our sexuality in later life.[11]

The emphasis on sexual intercourse as the ideal for sexuality in later life to the exclusion or downgrading of other forms of intimacy leads directly into another new myth: "Ageing causes sexual dysfunction and medical intervention is needed for older people to be sexually 'normal.'" Once again, sexual intercourse is the measure of what is sexually normal. Therefore, sexual dysfunction associated with old age is the inability to manage sexual intercourse. Problems such as erectile dysfunction and vaginal dryness, along with other physical limitations, are well known and frequently mentioned in the literature on old-age sexuality. That health care providers should provide medical solutions to deal with these problems is, she maintains, an ageist assumption that older people cannot be sexual without professional help.[12]

Another myth of the sexy oldie follows: "To be sexually attractive at any age you need to conform to a youthful standard of beauty (particularly if you are a woman)."[13] We met this problem in the last chapter—remember the song "Keep Young and Beautiful." We also saw that the same burden of youthful beauty can be shouldered by gay men, according to Ron Long's account. For Gott, the failure to maintain one's beauty as a woman means you can be sexually disenfranchised, desexualized. Moreover, "letting yourself go" can even socially disenfranchise a person. In short, to be sexually and socially acceptable, you have to find ways to minimize the physical effects of aging.

A final myth of the positive aging movement is that "sex in later life is pleasurable and an expression of love." This certainly sounds like a good statement on the face of it, and it is doubtless true for many older couples. However, Gott wants us to remember that the possibility for abuse and exploitation and sexual risk taking is also present among older adults. In some respects, as we shall see later in the narrative, certain of the harmful possibilities of sexual activity may be even more likely among older people. In any case, Gott wants us to recognize that the positive aging movement tends to overly romanticize old-age sexual activity while failing to include a recognition of the downsides. Not all sexual activity in later life will be a joy for everyone.[14]

In sum, the components of Gott's sexy oldie myth, she fears, are the makings of a new stereotype. While the positive aging philosophy seeks to liberate older people from ageist perceptions, they may have created a new myth that has them in the thrall of a sexualized version of old age.

The Positive and the Problematic

From a somewhat different perspective, Robert Youdin notes that psychologists still often hold to notions of old age as asexual. Thus a de facto ageism exists within the profession. And as noted in chapter 1, such ideas are also internalized by older people, who are consequently reluctant to seek the potentially helpful advice of *knowledgeable* health professionals about sexual matters. Recall Jennifer Hillman's case of the seventy-six-year-old woman that we reviewed in chapter 1. Citing a number of recent studies, Youdin goes on to say, "When older adults are questioned about their sexuality they report that they find sexual activity enjoyable and a source of pleasure, and a significant positive aspect of their lives. Sexuality is alive and well throughout all cohorts of older adults no matter how old."[15] This account provides us with another testimony to the durability of sexual interest and desire throughout the life span. It brings us back to the beginnings of this chapter and the positive indications of the AARP study, notwithstanding Gott's concern that the positive can become distorted into a negative.

Some studies report positive health benefits derived from continued sexual activity, including "decreased pain sensitivity, lower levels or no depression, a more positive view of intimate relationships, and consequent increased self-esteem."[16] Being in a marriage or partnered relationship has proved to be a good predictor of sexual satisfaction and activity among older adults: "Partnered older adult sexual activity remains the same between partners (relative to each partner) until at least age 74 (with 62.8% of women and 74.75% of men participating in sexual activity), and a significant decline in sexual activity begins between the ages of 75 and 84 (with 41.4% of women and 54.2% of men participating in sexual activity)."[17]

Once again, the sexual activities involved among these older adults cover the gamut of ways couples pleasure each other and express their intimacy. One might also note that though the study records a "significant decline" in sexual activity between the ages of seventy-five and eighty-four, a significant number of men and women are still sexually active in that age group. If we focus on the simple expressions of sexuality such as self-care, exchange of endearments, and simple displays of affectionate touch, I suspect the amount of active sexuality would be higher in the seventy-five- to eighty-four-year-old range than the studies report.

At the same time, there are problems that adversely affect the sexual lives of older adults. Diminished sexual activity due to the social and emotional burdens of poverty or financial distress, disability, or loss of one's sexual partner can lead to depression or anxiety in some older adults.[18] And as we have already noted, internalizing cultural stigmas or religious constraints can also play a part in older people's reticence to engage in sexual activities, perhaps in some cases to the detriment of their quality of life.

Before moving on, it is important to note that even as we focus on the continuing sexual desires and activities of older adults, there are many who for various physical, emotional, or contextual reasons have no desire to continue a sexual relationship.

Efforts to resolve the diminished capacity for sexual activity can sometimes have their downside. In a manner not unrelated to Gott's concern over health professionals' view on the necessity of medical intervention in the sex lives of older adults, Youdin speaks of the medicalization of sexuality with specific reference to oral medications for erectile dysfunction in older men. The pressure to perform and the use of medications to deal with erectile dysfunction cause "older men to be engaged in *virility surveillance*. Virility surveillance is represented by older adult men self-monitoring their sexual functioning, comparing it with their experiences from when they were young, and then determining that any deviation from their younger experiences is considered a sign of disordered sexual function."[19] The pressure to perform is intensified by the advertising industry's promotion of these products, which take their place alongside beauty products for women that claim to turn back the clock on the aging process. Marketing in this area often creates needs that don't exist—or at least needs that are not essential.

For theologian-ethicist Erin Dufault-Hunter, the medicalization of sex and its commercial promotion has created what she calls the "Viagra culture." The reliance on medication to deal with erectile dysfunction, she argues, has contributed to a resurgence of patriarchy: male dominance and the subordination of women. The emphasis on male sexual performance, which implies capacity for penetration, and the passivity of one's female partner can lead to a neglect of women's desires in their sexual lives. To the extent that this is true of the behavior of some men, it flies in the face of the Christian principles of self-giving and mutuality in love. Or, at least the allure of lifelong coitus can tempt men to be less sensitive and more self-centered. As one grows older, Dufault-Hunter maintains, men have the opportunity to embrace the realities of decline in sexual prowess and their new vulnerability and become more sensitive lovers.[20]

Not all men who use medication to deal with erectile dysfunction are necessarily insensitive lovers, and not all women who are their partners are necessarily unhappy about it. However, Dufault-Hunter's connection of the medicalization of sex to issues of patriarchy cannot be entirely discounted. Furthermore, patriarchy is an issue in the sexual lives of older women for other reasons. Women tend to live longer than men, leaving older women with fewer possible partners. Opportunities for older women are, then, further reduced by the tendency of older men to marry younger women. The numerical disadvantages women face in old age put men in the driver's seat. This, some would argue, is a recipe for a patriarchal context that is not favorable to the aspirations of older women for a satisfying relationship.[21] However, at the same time, women seventy-five to eighty-four, who outnumber men in that age group by nearly two to one, have found internet dating sites for seniors an avenue for finding new relationships. Sites for LGBT people are also available: "Due to the stigma typically faced by LGBT older adults, especially those who may be physically or socially isolated, online dating and social support can offer significant benefits."[22] The fact that over one million seniors use these dating sites is yet another indicator of the desire for companionship and intimacy in later life.

The Older LGBTQ Community: A Few Observations

Readers will have recognized that the research studies cited thus far have been exclusively heterosexual. We are all aware of the fact that sexuality, sexual orientation, and gender identity are now understood to be more complex and fluid than in the tradition of binary thinking. When it comes to aging and sexuality, there has been growth in research with respect to the LGBTQ community, but it has not achieved the same degree of attention given to heterosexuality and aging. We will have more to say about the lives of older LGBTQ adults when we discuss cohabitation and long-term care situations in the next two chapters. For the focus of this chapter, it is enough to say that sexual desire and sexual activities continue into old age across the spectrum of sexual orientation. Nonetheless, nonheterosexual adults seeking relationships of intimacy do face contextual problems that are not common to heterosexual couples.

Older gay and lesbian people, for example, "came out" at a time when homophobia was the norm in society. Unlike their younger postliberal peers, they have had to guard their identities and relationships from the censure of a disapproving social and religious context. Of course, that discrimination has not come to an end entirely. We daily see evidence of legal maneuvers to restrict the rights of LGBTQ persons in the workplace and divisive debates within church bodies over the acceptance of gay marriage and the moral status of same-sex relationships. So older gay and lesbian people have faced and still face a double whammy of the ageist disdain for old-age sexuality and heterosexist disdain for gay, lesbian, bisexual, and transgender sexuality and sexual relationships.

That said, here is an interesting twist. It is also the case that for some gay or lesbian couples, ageist assumptions about the asexuality of older people can be a benefit. That is, since those around them often assume these older couples aren't sexually active, seeing same-sex couples living together and in public together causes no homophobic anxiety. In Jennifer Hillman's study, one sixty-eight-year-old gay male reported, "I love being old now! No one bothers me or my lover anymore, even if we sit close when we go out walking or out to eat. It's like they think we have run out of steam or something, and that no one will bother us because we certainly can't bother them."[23] It is not uncommon for gay or lesbian persons to have previously been in a heterosexual relationship—perhaps with children from that partnership. The subsequent breakup does not always go well with family members. Bitterness and alienation sometimes follow the pain of loss. Sadly, I have witnessed this firsthand. At the same time, I have also seen situations where married couples stay together or part amicably after the disclosure occurs. In what seems a remarkable case, a couple who came to speak in one of my classes were still together in their marriage after the husband came out as a trans person and went through the lengthy process of sexual reassignment. The variety of responses human beings have to the manifold expressions of sexual relationships is certainly a challenge to pastoral care and in need of the kind of theologically informed ethical reflection we seek moving forward in this narrative.

Regardless of the circumstances of coming out, family acceptance and support are critical to the well-being of gay and lesbian persons throughout the life course. Rejection by family and contemporaries led older gay and lesbian people to develop support systems composed of their sexual peers. These "families of choice" can be of critical importance to the well-being of older gay and lesbian persons who may have no children to care for them and may be living alone. Forming such a community apart has also helped form a protective wall against discrimination.[24] For many, circles of friends or families of choice may prove more dependable than their actual family members:

> As an additional boon to gay elders who establish peer-related, social support networks, theorists suggest that friends may be a significantly better source of social support than family members. Compared to family members, friends are more likely to engage gay and lesbian elders in important life review discussions, including difficult or sensitive topics

> such as personal disappointments, fears of aging, and current and prior sexual relationships. Friends also are more likely to offer support and friendship because "they want to," whereas family members may offer assistance because they feel obligated or expected to. It often is easier to accept help from someone who gives it freely than from someone who extends help only because of perceptions that he or she has to.[25]

For some older gay and lesbian people, their intimate relationships with a partner were their only sustained means of personal support. Thus notwithstanding the greater acceptance of differences in sexual orientation, it will be particularly important for the Christian community, along with other faith communities, to provide affirmation and spiritual support for sexual identity and their partnerships.[26] These partnerships for older gay and lesbian folks have been in many cases lifelines in a world of disapproval. The support of the faith communities is particularly important, since churches have often been at the forefront of the oppression of gays and lesbians. For some faith communities who bear the name "Christian," this remains the case.

From Studies to Stories

The personal stories of those who participate in research studies are often elided or not presented in full. We all know older adults and older couples, sometimes within our extended family and sometimes among friends and acquaintances. However, the subject of personal sexual relationships is rarely if ever shared by our older family members or friends, though it is sometimes joked about. Joking about sex in old age strikes me as having the benefit of ambiguity; the listener is left to guess whether the joke is meant to suggest that the teller is still sexually active or to cover the fact that they aren't. There are, however, older people who are willing to share their personal stories. These accounts take us beyond what research reveals to a deeper appreciation of sexuality in later life.

Connie Goldman, a former staff member of National Public Radio and an independent public radio producer, has compiled stories of late-life love, her own and those of the twenty-two other couples she interviewed. Her interviews are of people in their seventies, eighties, and nineties. Like the studies we have looked at, their experiences help dispel ageist assumptions about love in later life. As she says pointedly, "Love, intimacy, sex, and meaningful relationships are not the exclusive domain of the young."[27]

Goldman provides us with accounts of relationships marked by compatibility, affection, compromise, adaptability, and a deep appreciation for the joy of finding new love in later life. Without exception, the participants had been previously married and either widowed or divorced. A number of the people say they had not seen a new relationship developing at this late stage in life but eagerly embraced it when it became possible. As one participant claims, "Companionship is essential."

The sex lives these folks reported run the gamut of what we associate with sexuality and intimacy: touching, hugging, kissing, cuddling, intercourse, and other forms of mutual pleasuring. Adjustments in lovemaking are made in the face of age-related limitations on sexual performance. "We make our way," says one woman. Whatever expressions of physical intimacy are practiced or possible, these people find their sex lives meaningful and pleasurable.

Initial concerns with body image in old age seem to dissipate as love and pleasure in one another take hold. One woman named Carole relates this revelation: "We have some kind of sexual activity three or four times a week. I don't have the greatest body, but to him my body is beautiful and that makes me feel wonderful. . . . We touch each other, hold each other. Sometimes it leads to sexual pleasure, sometimes it doesn't. . . . The satisfaction we take in our physical relationship is remarkable."[28]

Absent the distractions of child rearing and other family responsibilities, a number say that their sex lives are better than ever. An interviewee named Nicole says, "For me, physical intimacy is better than it has ever been in my whole life. Physical intimacy is a very important part of our relationship. We hug and kiss and touch a lot. When you have children, you're busy and distracted, and when you have babies, well, the sexual drive goes right down with the diapers." And her partner, Todd, adds, "When you're older, you see things differently . . . I've grown more patient and tolerant. I know I have a limited time left, and I'm more understanding and accepting."[29]

The preciousness of time in older age is a recurrent theme in these stories, and without exception, it generates a keen appreciation for the relationship one is blessed to have in the last years of life. Further, as Todd's comment suggests, long experience with our own frailties, failures, and finitude can make us more accepting of the other person's limitations—that is, if we are in the least bit capable of self-examination.

Keeping one's sex life in proper perspective, while yet caring deeply about it, is often characteristic of love in later life. In the case of Pat and John, the couple has had to contend with the aftermath of John's prostate cancer and the well-known limitations on sexual activity that often follow. They have adjusted. Frequent touch has now become important, pleasurable, and a joy. Pat reflects, "The essence of love is the sharing and the caring. It's the respect, the love, and the honor. It's not the heat of the passion. . . . Physicality is part of any couple's intimacy. I wouldn't want to live together and not have touch as part of our being together. But it's not the essence of our marriage. We have a very precious relationship that isn't defined solely by sex."[30]

A similar note was struck by Grace and Amelia, two older women who were previously married. They became friends and then became attracted to one another. Their relationship blossomed. Grace says, "It is wonderful to be with someone who is physically loving and demonstrative. Touching is very important in our relationship. It is beautiful and fulfilling . . . it doesn't have to manifest itself in the same way that heterosexual couples think of sexual activity. Loving and lovemaking aren't just about sex. Our culture doesn't understand this well."[31] Amelia and Grace also wonder whether being older makes them less concerned about what other people may think about their being together.

We will have the chance to visit a few of the other stories in Coleman's collection as well as vignettes from other sources as we move forward.

Checking on Our Agenda

At the beginning of chapter 1, we stated our goal: "To uphold the dignity of the aged and enable a deeper understanding and respect for their sexuality while providing an ethical account of Christian love that liberates and motivates as it engages the special issues of sexuality in later life." To that end, as a first step, we have examined the hurtful stereotypes of old age and old-age sexuality. We met them with a theological account that grounds the abiding dignity of life in all its stages—life created in the divine image, life ordained in baptism for a lifelong call to be God's people in the world. Created in the divine image of the Triune God, who is Love, we are created for love, the cornerstone of the ethical vision we are seeking.

A necessary step along the journey toward our goal, then, is to provide evidence that stereotypes and myths of old-age sexuality are not just hurtful; they are wrong. Therefore, this chapter has laid out the evidence that interest, desire, and activity in matters of sexuality continue into the last decades of life. While we recognize that this is not true of everyone, especially as they enter the fourth stage of life, a large percentage of those who are physically able and even some who are physically disabled express their sexuality in a variety of ways that are important to them. Given this evidence, a better-informed Christian community and all who are involved with older adults have an obligation to respect their sexuality and dignity and exercise greater sensitivity.

The research we have relied on in this chapter and the stories we looked at have been helpful for determining what is really going on in the sexual lives of older adults. The material displays respect for the sexuality and dignity of the people who are the subjects of research. The injustice of stereotypes is taken to task. There is respect for diversity in sexual identity along with concern for the pain of discrimination. In these ways, there is a clear humanistic "respect for persons," a basic premise in most ethical systems. *However,* in all the material we have looked at, no ethical judgments are offered regarding specific kinds of sexual activity or living arrangements.

To the extent that there is an ethical model at work in the research of these gerontologists and clinicians, I would say that it is implicitly what ethicists would call a teleological approach. That means that the right action or choice is the one that produces the greatest good for those involved as they understand it. Thus the sexual activities or relational arrangements older adults pursue are morally acceptable if they produce happiness and contribute to mental and physical well-being. In the next two chapters, we will also see faith-based reactions to the practices and policies of old-age sexuality in two highly visible arenas of sexual expression among older adults. This will set the table for our final work in bringing Christian faith active in love to bear upon the ethical issues of aging and loving.

Further Thoughts

There is a little Metro Park close to my home. It has lovely winding trails through a wooded nature preserve. I am out on those trails frequently. (I sometimes think of Christopher Robin's Hundred Acre Wood and half expect to come upon Winnie-the-Pooh at the next turn.) Not too long ago, when I was visiting with the excellent young naturalist at the nature center adjacent to the woods, I mentioned how much I enjoyed hiking in the woods. He allowed as to how those were "walking" trails, not hiking trails. I explained to him patiently that at my age, these are more than walking trails; they are "hiking" trails! Given a stiff back and arthritic joints, I proudly laid claim to the designation.

Years ago when I took to those trails, my body was more supple and my movements more fluid and effortless. Now I move along at a slower pace with more deliberate steps and enjoy the company of my old wooden walking stick. I am more patient with myself and more attentive to my body. But for all of that, the beauty of the woods is no less enjoyable and, I think, more appreciated as I consider how fortunate I am—fortunate to be able to continue soaking in this little corner of God's always surprising creation.

Well, perhaps we can risk an analogy and suggest that sexual intimacy in later life is "more like hiking." Adjustments are made to the physical limitations of age. We are more patient with each other and more attentive to our bodies. But for all of that, the shared pleasure is no less exquisite and maybe even more deeply appreciated as we think of how precious it is to give and receive touch and warmth in our latter days. This too is part of the beauty of God's always surprising creation.

Part Two

Engaging Reality

Chapter Three

LIVING OPTIONS AMONG OLDER ADULTS

> To all I would say how mistaken they are when they think that they stop falling in love when they grow old, without knowing that they grow old when they stop falling in love.
>
> —Gabriel García Márquez

Older adults are sexual beings with a desire to express their sexuality in everything from self-care, to self-pleasuring, to intimacy with another. It is the desire for intimacy and companionship, for loving and sharing, that captures our attention in this chapter.

COHABITATION: A GROWING PRACTICE

According to the April 2017 Pew Research Center report, the number of US adults cohabiting has risen by 75 percent among those over fifty during the past decade. This growth, driven mostly by the "baby boomers," has been faster than that of any other age group. Among cohabiters aged fifty years and older, the majority are in their fifties (57 percent). In the age group of sixty-five years and older, which is the focus of this book, three in ten are in their sixties, one in ten are in their seventies, and just 3 percent are in their eighties and older. Of those who are sixty-five and older, 27 percent are widowed, with the rest either divorced or never married.[1] Although the percentage in the oldest group is smaller at present, when the larger numbers in the younger cohort of the fifty-and-older population grow older, we will doubtless see an increase in the numbers of those cohabiting in the third and fourth stages of life. In other words, cohabitation and the issues it raises for the oldest cohort promise to be with us for the foreseeable future.

One reason for the rise of cohabitation in later life is the fact that fewer older adults are married. This means there is a larger pool of those eligible to cohabit. Several demographic trends have contributed to this growth in unmarried older adults. First, there has been a slight increase in people who never marry. Second, the rise in "gray divorce," involving folks aged fifty years or older, results in newly single individuals who increasingly choose to cohabit rather than marry. Finally, remarriage rates have declined 60 percent in recent decades and have stalled among older adults. Together, these factors signal an increase in the number of adults who could cohabit.[2] And as the Pew study demonstrates, large numbers of those eligible to cohabit in fact do. Indeed, cohabitation among those in this older group has grown remarkably in recent times and at a faster pace than might have been expected.

Why Cohabit?

Early research listed a number of economic and social benefits that accrue to cohabitation in later life. The cost-of-living advantages traditionally confined to marriage also can be achieved through cohabitation and without the legal obligations marriage involves. Couples can live together in a close, intimate relationship and pool their resources. By remaining unmarried, they are not legally responsible for the partner's medical expenses. Also, the partners do not have claims to each other's assets. Cohabitation enables couples to preserve their financial autonomy, ensuring that their wealth transfers to their offspring, if that is their will, rather than their partner. Furthermore, unmarried couples can continue to receive social security and pension benefits that may otherwise terminate upon remarriage.[3] While these financial considerations may well remain in the equation for those considering cohabitation in later life, a more recent study suggests that with the possible exception of protecting social security benefits, they are not of paramount importance for all cohabiters.[4]

There are a number of other reasons to cohabit in later life. Since cohabitation is not a settled institution like marriage with traditional norms and roles in place, couples are free to shape the relationship's dynamic and expectations according to their own desires. As one might expect, this process can create conflict and disagreement. However, it is also an opportunity for couples to create an alternative relationship that fulfills or seeks to fulfill their respective needs and mutual desires. So, for example, some studies have observed that women may favor cohabitation because it does not entail the gendered caregiving obligations typical of traditional marriage. Therefore, it is alleged, cohabitation can allow women a greater opportunity to preserve their autonomy.[5]

A number of studies combine to provide further insight into cohabitation among older adults, which, in the minds of some, may add to the attractiveness or acceptance of cohabitation in later life:

> The meaning or purpose of later life cohabitation is unique. Whereas cohabitation among young adults tends to operate as a prelude to marriage or an alternative to singlehood, culminating in either marriage or separation within a year or two of its inception, cohabitation among older adults functions as a long-term alternative to marriage. The relationship quality and stability of older cohabiters exceeds that of younger cohabiters, even though older cohabiters are relatively unlikely to report plans to marry their partners. Indeed, cohabitation in later life tends to be quite stable, with an average duration of nearly ten years.
>
> Only a minority of older cohabiting couples wed or break up. Rather, the most common union outcome for older cohabiters is dissolution resulting from the death of the partner. The relationship dynamics of later life cohabitation are akin to remarriage.[6]

The fact that cohabitation in later life is marked by greater stability and longer duration than cohabitation among younger people could be an important factor when we come to a discussion of the morality of cohabitation versus marriage in old age.

Another study of interest indicates that the quality of life among older cohabiters is commensurate with that of older married people. Measures for quality of life in comparing cohabiting and those married or remarried were *happiness*, *emotional satisfaction*, *pleasure*, *openness*, and *time together*. Although those cohabiting were somewhat less likely to say they were happy, the results in all the other measures were almost the same. In terms of the negative indicators tested, *criticism* and *demands*, those cohabiting fared better.[7]

Personal testimonies put flesh on the bones of these research findings. Again, Connie Goldman's interviewees provide us with some samples. One case tells the story of a couple in their seventies, both widowed, who met, fell in love, and moved in together. In their situation, his lawyer told him not to get married, and her financial advisor gave the same advice. Financial considerations and relations with the children make it too complicated to get legally married, they said. Also, in this particular case, the woman had been and remained a continuing source of support for her autistic son. Her concern was that if they were married and her new husband became seriously ill, their joint resources in marriage could be depleted by his care, leaving her unable to support her autistic son.[8] For some, if not many, choosing cohabitation rather than marriage is not simply a matter of protecting income or inheritance; the decision is tied up with other needs that are unique to each situation.

In a somewhat similar fashion, a seventy-eight-year-old in a committed relationship says he does not want to marry and turn what is a daily voluntary arrangement into a compulsory legal contract. "Why," he asks, "should we spend a great deal of time trying to deal with money and inheritance issues that would be involved with our two families?" Being unmarried but strongly committed to another person avoids these problems. At the same time, as an expression of their mutual agreement, this couple is preparing themselves financially for the caregiving challenges and costs that will come as the physical limitations of age intrude.[9] For them, avoiding the financial entailments of marriage is a matter of simplicity versus complexity. Keeping it simple serves the integrity of their personal bond, which is unalloyed by a legal agreement. At the same time, the seriousness of their dedication is signaled by their readiness to prepare for the mutual caregiving that will likely come.

In addition to financial considerations, children's feelings can also be a factor in the decision not to remarry. Children may accept friendship, affection, and love in a new relationship for their parent, but not marriage. One man reflects that too often, he has seen children resent the claim a new spouse has on their parent's affection and money. He can't predict that his own children would react that way, but he does not want to take the risk.[10] New relationships in later life will often involve the adult children of both partners. A good relationship with one's adult children in later life is hard to overvalue. Protecting the health of those relations is of paramount importance. Their children's support for whatever decision couples make can be a determining factor in their choice.

Some responses to why people cohabit are simply subjective and stated as matters of conviction: "I don't need to be married. I love being with [him]. We're partners. I know that, so I don't know what the advantage would be to be married. My ninety-three-year-old mother talks to me as if I'm the most sinful woman on earth. . . . She has traditional values; she'd prefer we were married but has come to accept my choice of not being married."[11]

Another witness simply says, "One of the biggest mistakes someone can make after their husband or wife dies is to remarry too quickly. Find a partner but don't get married. Don't give in to social pressures or allow anyone to make you feel like you're living in sin. Every couple should make their own decisions about what they are comfortable with." This person hastens to add that despite being unmarried, he and his partner care for each other, as he had done faithfully in the aftermath of his wife's stroke.[12] This person seems to be saying, without apology, that the freedom of personal choice trumps the expectations of social and religious conventions. However, he also wants people to know that this is not simply a defiant, selfish choice. Rather, he and his partner are faithful to what all would agree are responsible love demands.

Living Together Apart

Living together but not in the same residence might be considered a subset of cohabitation. The couple has made a mutual commitment to be long-term partners in life and to share the same sort of intimacy one would expect in marriage. Living apart in close proximity may mean having an agreed-upon schedule for being with each other in one residence for a time and then switching. Occasionally, those who have entered into what they consider a committed relationship may live at some distance, making the opportunities to be together somewhat less frequent but nonetheless regular.

The reasons for this kind of alternative living arrangement vary. For some, retaining the security of their own residence in the face of advancing age and uncertain longevity is a primary consideration, especially if children have a stake in the disposition of that property after their parent's death. When one is late in life, the idea of picking up and moving, perhaps from a house that has been in the family for many years, may seem personally and emotionally unthinkable. A house that the children call home is hard to divest. There are various personal and financial reasons people become deeply invested in a particular place and therefore reluctant to let go of it. If the relationship is one in which the two live in different communities at some distance from each other, living together in the same house will mean a major move that could involve the loss of long-standing community ties and friendships—not to mention the cost of moving.

Staying apart yet being together in an intimate relationship may appeal to older adults in terms of retaining their financial independence. They pay their own bills and keep their financial planning and obligations separate from each other, thereby avoiding the complications of shared day-to-day money matters that go with the running of a household. Also, for some personalities, this arrangement might make it easier to tolerate habits and traits that would be off-putting on a daily basis. Just maintaining one's privacy after a long life, free from the scrutiny of a live-in partner, can be important for some who have lived with a spouse for many years.

Older lesbians and older gay males have chosen in many cases not to legalize their partnerships for financial reasons common to couples in the heterosexual world. However, a 2011 study in the United Kingdom shows the proportion of older lesbian, gay, and bisexual partners living apart to be three times as great as heterosexual older people with the same living arrangement. (They did have the option of registering for a civil partnership. Same-sex marriage became legal in the UK in 2014.) In an interview with an older lesbian called Joan, the researcher, Jane Traies, sheds some light on at least one reason for this difference between the two populations.[13]

Joan and her partner were prominent members of a Christian congregation. This affected their choice of living arrangement as a couple. Joan says, "We decided categorically that we would not live together because we thought that wouldn't be a good idea as far as the church was concerned. They would look and say, 'Ah, well, you know. They were very good friends!'" Joan and her partner's decision to live apart in order to conceal the nature of their relationship is not unique.[14] As we noted in the previous chapter, despite progress in the acceptance of LGBTQ persons and the legalization of same-sex marriage, the disdain and censure for all who are not heterosexual remains a toxic reality in certain circles, even certain church circles. So it is not surprising when a couple from within the LGBTQ community chooses the same course of action as Joan and her partner did.

One might surmise that heterosexual couples could also live apart for similar reasons. Though they don't face the same discrimination as a gay or lesbian couple might, they may also wish to avoid any expression of disapproval from members of their faith community. Perhaps they simply do not wish to have to explain their life choices to anyone. Living an alternate lifestyle can open one to raised eyebrows and meaningful silences. Living apart keeps things less visible to judgmental eyes. Even if it is not the primary consideration, a measure of invisibility may be an appealing aspect of the choice to live together but apart.

Cohabitation: A *Growing* Concern? Voices from Christian Communities

Cohabitation and its alternate form of living together but apart have become growing concerns among Christian church leaders. It is time in this narrative to hear some of the voices from Christian communities.

Roman Catholics on Cohabitation

As with most church bodies, Catholic opposition to cohabitation is framed in defense of marriage. The United States Conference of Catholic Bishops (USCCB) condemns cohabitation in the context of its pastoral letter on marriage. Sexual intercourse outside of marriage is gravely immoral because the natural purpose of sexual intercourse can only be realized in the permanent commitment of marriage.[15]

David Matzko McCarthy, a professor of Catholic social thought at Mount Saint Mary's University, echoes the view of the USCCB: "The institutional and communal foundation of marriage—the vows, expectations, and social relationships structured on the basis of family, the social tasks of sustaining productive households, and the common callings of raising children—give marriage purposes that an interpersonal relationship cannot sustain."[16]

Todd A. Salzman and Michael G. Lawler recognize the fact that cohabitation is widespread among Catholic couples prior to presenting themselves for marriage. For those cohabiting Catholics who do intend to marry, Salzman and Lawler propose that the church look at cohabitation in their cases as part of a four-step process culminating in marriage. The first step is betrothal, involving a ritual of pledging intent to marry. The second step is "nuptial cohabitation," which means living together and enjoying marital and sexual intercourse. The third step is fertility, allowing for the conception and birth of children. The final step is the wedding, when the couple has been able to overcome the socioeconomic restrictions that society had placed upon them. This process, they argue, fulfills the church's insistence that sexual intercourse happen only within the context of a stable marriage. The key is the interpersonal relationship of commitment throughout the process. This is the moral basis of this approach to nuptial cohabitation—rather than a single act of a marriage ceremony and a single act of sexual consummation.[17]

This is an interesting and rather progressive—or at least, pastorally sensitive—approach to cohabitation. Their proposal is clearly aimed at the church's response to younger couples who are cohabiting. It would be a strange suggestion if applied to the older adults of our discussion. However, I include it for several reasons. First, it does in its own way reiterate the church's opposition to what Salzman and Lawler would call nonnuptial cohabitation—a judgment, one can readily infer, that would also fall upon older cohabiters who do not intend marriage. We should also note that this discussion is decidedly related only to heterosexual couples; the Catholic Church would not recognize or accept any form of same-sex union.

The second reason is their emphasis on the interpersonal relationship as the true context for judging the morality of decisions and actions. Personal commitments of fidelity and justice sustain the morality of living together and enjoying one another sexually until external impediments to marriage are overcome. The first question this prompts is, "Is it possible that older adults who are cohabiting can be affirmed by the church simply on the basis of interpersonal commitments of fidelity, love, and justice, recognizing that overcoming the impediments to marriage, external and personal, may be an extraneous consideration under the conditions of old age?" Second, the physicalism of the USCCB's focus on the act of sexual intercourse outside marriage as that which makes cohabitation immoral raises interesting questions for seniors whose sexual intimacy may not include actual sexual intercourse. These questions, if not in direct response to the Catholic position, will in some form or another make their way into our agenda.

Other Conservative Christians Weigh In

The rationale (*whereas* statements) given by the Southern Baptist Convention in 2009 for a number of stands on sexuality and public policy makes clear their views on the Bible and sexual behavior:

ON BIBLICAL SEXUALITY AND PUBLIC POLICY

WHEREAS, From the beginning, the Bible establishes the basis for sexuality by declaring that human beings are created in God's image as "male and female" (Genesis 1:26–27) and that "a man leaves his father and mother and bonds with his wife, and they become one flesh" (Genesis 2:24); and

WHEREAS, Jesus answered questions about marriage by reaffirming this male/female and "one flesh" creation pattern for sexuality (Matthew 19:4–6); and

WHEREAS, The Apostle Paul based his teaching about marriage upon God's creation order of this one man/one woman relationship and the analogy of Christ and His bride, the Church (Ephesians 5:29–31); and

WHEREAS, Any sexual behavior outside of this husband/wife marriage relationship is sinful, including premarital sex, adultery, bestiality, and pornography (Hebrews 13:4; Galatians 5:19; 1 Corinthians 6:9–11; Leviticus 18:23); and

WHEREAS, Homosexual behavior is specifically prohibited and condemned in both the Old and New Testaments (Genesis 19:1–27; Leviticus 18:22; Romans 1:18–25; 1 Corinthians 6:9–11).[18]

While the resolution that follows does not speak of cohabitation, the biblical theology of sexuality and marriage laid out in the *whereas* statements precludes any positive assessment of cohabitation along with any form of same-sex union. Professor Evan Lenow, who teaches ethics at the Southwestern Baptist Theological Seminary in Fort Worth, Texas, makes this quite clear: "Those who cohabit participate in the 'pleasures' of the relationship without the covenantal commitment. This stands in direct violation of God's plan for marriage that He established in Genesis 2 prior to the Fall." He goes on to say that the church's ministry to those cohabiting is to urge them to repent of their sin, ideally in the presence of the church, and separate from their sinful relationship.[19]

Focus on the Family is self-described on its website as an "American fundamentalist Christian organization." It was founded in 1977 in Southern California by James Dobson and is based in Colorado Springs, Colorado. In their internet posting entitled "Cohabiting Senior Couples: Financial and Moral Considerations," they offer this case:

> Is it wrong for seniors to live together for financial reasons? My elderly father recently moved in with a woman he's been dating for several months. When I objected, he told me that they had discussed marriage many times but ultimately rejected the idea for financial reasons. According to my dad, it's a matter of protecting their individual assets and preserving each partner's Social Security benefits. He says they would actually lose a sizable portion of their monthly income if they were to get married. Now

he's talking about having a "commitment ceremony" at church as an alternative to legal marriage. What's your take on this? Does the Bible have anything to say about a couple being married in the eyes of the church but not according to the laws of the state?[20]

In response, Focus on the Family argues that marriage is communal, not just private, because it has profound implications for the well-being of society. God has given marriage as part of common grace for all people. Marriage is an ordinance not simply of the church but also of the government, which God has established for our good (Romans 13:1–7). Therefore, it is incumbent upon Christians to honor the marriage laws the state has established. Should older adults be excused from marriage for financial reasons, then younger adults, they argue, should have the same privilege. Accordingly, "if a man and a woman *at any stage of life* really love one another enough to become 'one flesh' in the eyes of God, they should be willing to proclaim their mutual commitment to the world. They should do this in the presence of the governing authorities and society as a whole by entering into legal matrimony. It doesn't matter what this commitment may cost them in terms of money or material comforts. In the end, it comes down to a simple question of doing the right thing."

The interesting thing about this response is that it does not speak directly of the moral issue of sex outside of marriage, or "living in sin." Of course, that may be inferred, but instead, Focus on the Family stresses the communal nature of marriage as divinely ordered and not satisfied by anything less than public, legal legitimation of the relationship; a church commitment ceremony won't do. This response leads us directly into the next resource I want to discuss and into a point we will need to address.

Irma Fast Dueck, an associate professor at the Canadian Mennonite University, has written a probing article on cohabitation and marriage. Dueck recognizes the increase in cohabitation, particularly among the young. She recognizes that cultural norms have shifted; sex outside of marriage has become acceptable to more and more people inside and outside the church. She also recognizes that most opposition to cohabitation is made in defense of marriage. Dueck then provides a helpful analysis of the fact that the nature and form of marriage have changed due to cultural influences throughout its history. Marriage and the nuclear family of today, she maintains, is not a form and understanding directly out of the Bible but one shaped by the social patterns of the Industrial Revolution. Thus we need to take a critical look at reigning notions of marriage and the theology of marriage before we can establish the basis of the church's critique of cohabitation.[21] What, then, distinguishes marriage from cohabitation? This is Dueck's answer:

> Perhaps the feature that most distinguishes marriage from cohabitation is community. At its best, marriage is a community-building act from the outset, while cohabitation is not. Love and commitment are promised publically in the presence of family and friends and the church. Marriage begins in the context of a community and from the start acknowledges that we are part of a larger human family. It recognizes that one's life is more than one's own, that one's actions affect more than oneself and one other. It in essence proclaims that marriage is more than a private affair between two people; it finds its meaning in the context of a broader community, the church, the body of Christ.[22]

Living together without marriage, by contrast, conveys the idea that this couple's life choice is nobody's business but their own. There is no communal involvement or blessing; it is simply a private matter.[23]

In the end, Dueck's main concern is ministry to younger people considering or practicing cohabitation. However, her stress on the communal nature of marriage versus the private character of cohabitation is not unlike the brief response in the Focus on the Family posting. The emphasis on communal accountability and the contribution public marriage makes to the stability and mutuality of community life lead us back to the theology of vocation introduced in chapter 1. There I affirmed the lifelong ordination to the ministry of the whole people of God, a vocation given in baptism that continues to both dignify and obligate people until their final days. Marriage is certainly a state for the expression of that vocation. Is it, then, an obligation for seniors in order to be true to their baptismal calling? Is the Christian churches' concern for the importance of marriage dealt a blow by the witness of its older members choosing not to marry though living together?

These questions have been lurking since the start of our discussion of cohabitation. They go with us as we proceed.

Lutheran Voices

The Lutheran Church–Missouri Synod, on its official website, has published a substantial statement, "Living Together without Marriage."[24] The statement begins with a brief biblical account of marriage as ordained by God in creation (Genesis 2:24; Matthew 19:5–6; Ephesians 5:31) and sustained in the New Testament as God's precious blessing. It should be honored by all and kept pure (Hebrews 13:4), the very picture of Christ's relationship with his bride the church (Ephesians 5:22–33). They believe it logically follows that it is wrong to live together without marriage because to do so is against God's clear Word, which has established marriage as the norm for the unity of man and woman. More specifically, the statement cites the sixth commandment against adultery, claiming that living together without marriage is just that. In support of that claim, they quote Luther's explanation to the sixth commandment: "We should fear and love God so that we lead a sexually pure and decent life in what we say and do; and husband and wife love and honor each other." In other words, they conclude, men and women should not live together as husband and wife unless they truly are husband and wife. Pointedly, they say, "This is as true for 80-year-olds as it is for 18-year-olds."

Robert W. Weise, professor of practical theology at Concordia Seminary in St. Louis, writing from his Missouri Synod Lutheran position on behalf of marriage, also rejects cohabitation in all circumstances: "Cohabitation of all age groups as a foundation for future marriages builds on sinking sand rather on the rock, Jesus Christ, the Son of the living God. . . . Cohabitation is neither acceptable nor permitted by the word of God, regardless of the couple's reason(s) for living together."[25]

The Evangelical Lutheran Church in America (ELCA) adopted a major social statement, *Human Sexuality: Gift and Trust*, at its 2009 Churchwide Assembly. *Vocation* and *trust* are key terms in this document. It states, "Central to our vocation, in relation to human sexuality, is the building and protection of trust in relationships."[26] This vocation to build relationships of trust is not a private matter; it is part of the Christian witness in the community and the Christian's calling in all situations.[27]

The statement's advocacy for marriage as a venue for Christian vocation is framed as the context for the building and sustaining of trust and mutuality: "The trust and mutuality afforded by marriage can make marriage one of the most beautiful, abiding, and transformative forms of human relationship. . . . Sexual intimacy, together with promises of fidelity and public accountability, nurtures bonds that allow people to thrive and provides a rich context for the care and support of children."[28] Moreover, this public character of marriage, expressed through a legal contract, implies civil responsibility and is a source of strength to the community by its witness of mutual trust and fidelity.[29]

When it comes to cohabitation, the ELCA recognizes the social forces that fuel cohabitation, such as an increase in the number of failed marriages, the social acceptance of casual sex, and a culture of individualism not given to social responsibility and accountability. They also realize there are economic pressures that work against legal marriage. Here they mention the impact of economic hardships involved in marriage for older adults explicitly. The church should then work to alter laws and other factors that create impediments to marriage. However, if the decision to cohabit is made, regardless of the reasons, the church expects its pastors to convey the church's clear conviction that "the deepest longings for a sense of personal worth, long-term companionship, and profound security, especially given the human propensity to sin, are best served through binding commitment, legal protections, and the public accountability of marriage."[30]

The ELCA statement falls short of condemning people who cohabit as living in sin; rather, they are referred to pastoral care. But it stresses even more strongly the communal nature of our sexual relations and the building of trust not only within the relationship but also as a matter of public trust. All this is a function of our God-given vocation, which is once again a persistent concern to be addressed in discussing cohabitation.

THE EPISCOPAL CHURCH USA

Proposals and conversations about cohabitation in the Episcopal Church are some of the most interesting and progressive among American church bodies. The church's Task Force on the Study of Marriage, in recognition of the increasing numbers of people cohabiting and what they considered the inadequacy of former teachings on sex outside of marriage, proposed the following resolution to the 2018 General Convention:

> **Resolution 2018-A086**
>
> *Resolved*, That "The Blessing of a Lifelong Relationship" shall not be used for mere convenience. It may be used 1) by couples who desire to form and to formalize a relationship with one another that is monogamous, unconditional and lifelong, but is nevertheless something different than a marriage in that it does not include the merging of property, finances or other legal encumbrances; and 2) by couples for whom the requirement to furnish identification to obtain a marriage license could result in legal penalties including deportation, because of their immigration status; and be it further
>
> *Resolved*, That these rites are to be used under the direction of a bishop exercising ecclesiastical authority; and be it further
>
> *Resolved*, That it shall be within the discretion of any Member of the Clergy of this Church to decline to officiate at any rite of blessing defined herein;

The resolution continues then to assure that no repercussions be suffered by those clergy who in conscience refuse to use this rite and that the rite be added to the church's liturgical resource, "Enriching Our Worship."[31]

As the resolution suggests, financial and other impediments to legal marriage may be behind the choice of this route for the blessing of one's relationship. Furthermore, it is clear that the relationship in question should embody the same sorts of morally binding commitments one would expect in marriage. It is a course of action born of necessity, not mere convenience.

The convention response to resolution A086 leaves its enactment in abeyance: "*Resolved*, That the 79th General Convention refer 'The Blessing of a Lifelong Relationship' (as appended to the report of the Task Force on the Study of Marriage) to the Standing Commission on Liturgy and Music and the Standing Commission on Structure, Governance, Constitution and Canons for further review and recommendations including a comprehensive study of the legal implications and other ecclesial options."[32]

The fact that this resolution is still under discussion is a noteworthy initiative among church bodies, mainline and otherwise. The theological discussion surrounding this proposal to bless cohabiting relationships deserves our attention. An essay on households attached to the task force "Blue Book Report" to the convention provides some insight into the sort of thinking involved in resolution A086.

The idea of a household as community is modeled after the relational, communal nature of the Trinity in the giving and receiving of love. The sharing of communal living enhances the love for one another and the love that overflows into the world in service and love of neighbor. To quote the task force, "Whether the household is formed by marriage, cohabitation, parenting, or in some other way . . . the intimacies that come from close contact can create networks of trust and mutuality in which the fruit of the Spirit can be known and shared."[33] It is not uncommon for older adults cohabiting, even if living apart, to think of themselves as "married in the sight of God," given their commitments to fidelity, love, and justice as Christian people who wholeheartedly embrace these concomitants of the love Christ demands. The proposed liturgy for "The Blessing of a Lifelong Relationship" seeks to formalize that conviction in the presence of the church.

For the Episcopal Church, marriage is a sacrament that is taken with the same high degree of seriousness and sense of holiness we could hope to find in any other Christian church body. However, rather than defending marriage against the problematic reality of cohabitation, it seems that cohabitation has become a separate entity alongside marriage. It can be construed as one form of "householding" along with others, sharing in common obligations of love for one another that is analogous to the love that is the Trinity. The resolution does say that this liturgy is for the blessing of a lifelong relationship that *is something different* from marriage. At this writing, the Episcopal Church has yet to affirm this resolution and the theology behind it. Yet it is being treated with seriousness and respect.

Updating the Agenda

Thus far, we have been confronted with a variety of questions about cohabitation in later life. Is it, regardless of the circumstances prompting it, still "living in sin"? Does cohabitation undercut the communal witness of marriage and public accountability that is so important for social stability? Therefore, is cohabitation at any stage of life a failure of our baptismal vocation to live a life worthy of our calling (Ephesians 4:1)? On the other hand, is it possible that older adults who are cohabiting can be affirmed by the church simply on the basis of interpersonal commitments of fidelity, love, and justice, recognizing that overcoming the impediments to marriage, external and personal, may be extraneous considerations under the conditions of old age? If we answer in the affirmative, are we led to something like the ritual of blessing under discussion in the Episcopal Church—perhaps the creation of a new ritual for a new category of union alongside marital union that can be considered equally holy?

Regardless of what we have just seen from various church traditions, here is an excerpt from a 2019 Pew Research Center survey recording the views of their members:

> About three-quarters of Catholics (74%) and white Protestants who do not self-identify as born-again or evangelical (76%) say it's acceptable for an unmarried couple to live together even if they don't plan to get married. By contrast, only 47% of black Protestants and 35% of white evangelical Protestants share this view. And while half or more across these groups say society is better off if couples who want to stay together long-term eventually get married, white evangelicals are the most likely to say this (78% do so). Among those who are not religiously affiliated, fully nine-in-ten say cohabitation is acceptable even if a couple doesn't plan to get married, and just 31% say society is better off if couples who want to stay together eventually get married.[34]

The attitudes expressed by the survey do not distinguish between cohabitation among the young and middle-aged and cohabitation among older adults in the third and fourth stages of life. That is our job. This survey is about all forms of cohabitation. So the important point is that the percentages of Catholics and white Protestants who approve of cohabitation regardless of plans to marry are close to those of nonreligious respondents. How, if at all, will these responses among parishioners affect the future teaching of church leaders and theologians on the matter? When it comes to morality, especially sexual morality, efforts to adapt to new realities have often brought the accusation that a secularizing culture is setting the church's agenda, whereas the church should be countercultural in fidelity to Scripture and tradition.

Theology and Christian ethics have always been engaged in navigating the interplay of (1) *biblical authority*, which involves an understanding of its revelatory core, cultural, and historical setting; (2) *doctrinal tradition*, established in the ecumenical creeds and continually evolving through history in the response to the challenges of each new context; (3) *experience* shared by and among the faithful concerning their life encounters under various conditions both as individuals and as members of a particular group; (4) *culture*, the custom, institutions, and philosophical influences shaping the contexts of life in any given time and place; and (5) *reason* in the service of sound analysis and logical communication and as expressed in the findings and theories of the social, psychological, and medical sciences. These sources have already emerged in our discussion and will continue to be in dialogue to the end.

Further Thoughts

Beauty

I suspect most of us at one time or another have had unkind thoughts upon seeing a couple who appeared mismatched in physical beauty. Not knowing them personally, we muse, I wonder what she sees in him? *or* I wonder what he sees in her? *Such thoughts express a very superficial appraisal of beauty but, nonetheless, fit the general attitude that appearance is the most common measure of beauty or attractiveness. They also point us to the fact that beauty is a highly subjective matter. "Beauty is in the eyes of the beholder" means just that: beauty is not an objective quality inherent in the person or thing observed but a subjective quality in the perception of the observer.*

Subjective, yes, but the concept of beauty is still under the sway of cultural norms of attractiveness when it comes to human beings. While concepts of beauty certainly differ among societies, in our Western culture, the ideals of youthful femininity and masculinity that prevail in the media set the standard in the public arena. This, we have already observed, feeds an ageist assumption that the faded beauty of old age equates to a faded sexual life.

The February 2020 edition of National Geographic *has a major article entitled "Redefining Beauty." As the title suggests, the piece unveils a broadening definition of beauty within and across cultural lines. At the same time, it admits that the narrower standards of youthful beauty still render their dehumanizing judgments on those who do not fit the mold: "We have come to equate beauty with humanity. If we don't see the beauty in another person, we are blind to that person's humanity."*[35] *However, though the cult of youth remains a burden on the self-esteem of many, there does seem to be some hope of a change in thinking about beauty, a change toward an attitude of respect for the right to exist as you are and to be seen for the beauty in you as you are. Thus "when an older woman's wrinkles are seen as beautiful, it means that she is actually being seen. She isn't being overlooked as a full human being: sexual, funny, smart, and, more than likely, deeply engaged in the world around her" (p. 114). In a similar vein, perhaps, a good friend of mine who is in her late seventies speaks of being liberated from the burdens of youth's expectations of physical perfection, thereby finding that beauty is internal, a gracious quality that comes to life in relationships, intimate and otherwise.*

I'm prompted by these thoughts to pursue the idea of redefining beauty a bit further. I'll start with this definition of beauty *from* Merriam-Webster's Collegiate Dictionary*: "the quality or aggregate of qualities in a person or thing that gives pleasure to the senses or pleasurably exalts the mind or spirit."*

This definition suggests to me that there are qualities we find beautiful that take us beyond only the visual perception to the experience of the whole person in relationship: an "aggregate of qualities" that can appeal to all our senses.

In old age, people often experience in each other a kind of spiritual beauty born of life experience, a quality of mature character that is attractive and compelling. Years of loving and caring clothe a person with the sort of beauty that can only come from a lifetime of faithful self-giving and self-sharing. The beauty of winsome expressions and kindness, tenderness, humor—each has an endearing quality of attractiveness that is an enduring source of delight for those who are close to them. Maybe these qualities captivate because of their well-traveled humanity. The warmth of bodies entwined is a quality that gives intense pleasure and deep satisfaction, an aesthetic experience that remains very real in later life. The wrinkled skin of age still yields the softness of loving touch. The qualities that sustain the manifold and diverse expressions of beauty in later life are all the more appreciated as precious gifts. They are the graces that anticipate the experience of ultimate beauty in the presence of God who is love.

> The glory of youths is their strength,
> but the beauty of the aged is their grey hair.
>
> —Proverbs 20:2

Chapter Four

Sexual Life in Long-Term Care Facilities

> There are men and women so lonely, they believe God, too, is lonely.
>
> —Carl Sandberg

> Warmth, closeness, and touching with another resident can alleviate the profound loneliness that affects many long-term care residents.
>
> —Robin Dessel, Hebrew Home at Riverdale

Cohabiting couples may in some cases feel the burden of scrutiny by family, church, or community, but basically, they are free to conduct their lives together as they please and in the privacy of their own homes. However, for those living in long-term care or assisted living facilities and nursing homes, unrestricted privacy and complete freedom of choice in matters of one's sexual life are not guaranteed. Institutional policies and priorities, staff attitudes, and family involvement may in various ways intrude upon a resident's desires and felt needs. At the same time, it is in long-term care venues that physical and mental health issues are most prominent. These features of advanced age not only impose limitations on sexual expression but also present challenges for staff in the administration of health care, maintenance of safety standards, and prevention of abuse.

Upholding the dignity of the aged as adult persons and sexual beings under the complex conditions of institutional life requires special efforts of understanding, sensitivity, and respect. So we proceed with this chapter deeply appreciative of those caregivers who work hand in hand with the elderly in long-term care and with the hope that what follows will be helpful to them and those in their care.

> Snow on the mountain, fire in the furnace—just because I'm old don't mean the other parts of me aren't hot.

This colorful quote reminds us of what by now should come as no surprise: the elderly continue to have sexual desires that don't disappear when they take up residence in a long-term care home. In their study of sexual intimacy in assisted living facilities, Ann Christine Frankowski and Leanne J. Clark report that sexual activity among married couples and single men and women runs the gamut of everything from intercourse to various forms of intimate contact, including cuddling, hand-holding, flirting, self-pleasuring, and self-care.[1] Furthermore, as we have observed earlier, it is clear that future cohorts of older adults can be expected to have even higher sustained interest in sex and also a greater frequency of sexual activity. It is a generally accepted fact that their generation will come with a potentially greater acceptance of the idea that sexual activity in old age is normal and healthy. What is already the reality of vital sexual life in long-term care communities only promises to grow in the immediate future.

Despite the negative influences of physical and psychological ill health and the consequences of normal aging, it is nonetheless clear that older people continue to be sexually active and enjoy the physical and psychological benefits of this. For older people with heart failure, sex may be seen as less important, but studies show no significant difference in their overall interest in sex compared with healthy older adults. There also appears to be no difference in sexual interest levels between older (aged over sixty-four years) and younger women. Older people in residential care both with and without dementia still consider sexual intimacy to be important.[2] Indeed, intimacy can be essential to overcoming the loneliness that can overtake people in long-term care settings, a loneliness that is not always offset by interactions in community activities.[3]

It is not surprising, then, that a recent review of research on the relationship between long-term care residents and health care professionals underscores the need for health care professionals to acknowledge and uphold the importance of sexuality in older age. This can be achieved, it is argued, by enabling open discussions about sexuality with older people. Some professionals think it is good to incorporate an appreciation and understanding of sexuality into treatment and care planning. Add to this the need to facilitate the creation of long-term care environments that provide discreet sexual opportunities for older people for whom this is important. This review highlights that it is important for health care professionals to have strong and effective communication skills, and they should be interested, understanding, concerned, and empathetic. However, as far as the authors of this review are concerned, the evidence is clear that communication between older people and health care professionals about sexual issues is in need of improvement.[4] This accords with a conclusion reached by another study: "Older people are uncomfortable and reluctant to raise sexuality and sexual health issues due to negative perceptions of the health-care professional's interests and attitudes."[5]

Intimacy requires privacy. The physical accommodations of many facilities may make privacy a difficult thing to achieve. People may have roommates. Staff may enter as they knock rather than knocking before they enter. Couples may need special arrangements to spend time together in private. There may not be dedicated private spaces available for couples to share.

If communication with health care professionals and environmental accommodations can be problematic for the sexual aspirations of long-term care residents, interactions with family can also be an issue. Respect for their autonomy and its corollary, privacy, are essential to the intimacy of older adults in long-term care settings. Though the facility's administration may seek to ensure that these rights are in place, family reactions and actions may compromise this commitment. The following example illustrates this kind of family intervention.

The executive director of an assisted living facility explained that they inform the family when a sexual relationship becomes evident so there won't be any surprises or gossip. She added that children can become very upset because "Mom was never like this"; they are embarrassed. In one instance, a daughter came at lunchtime, caught her mother with "that person," and was appalled. She said, "Mom, you came here like the Virgin Mary." So the director went on to explain that the administration is forced to balance the rights of the residents with the strong views of family members. However, the family may, if they are not satisfied, move their relative to another facility, leaving an empty room or suite and loss of revenue. So the desires and rights of the resident can at times be at the mercy of the family and its ability to exert economic pressure to get its way—this despite the fact that the family has no right to interfere. Thus we have yet another example of the general demeaning attitude that disregards the sexuality of older adults, even on the part of their families.[6]

In addition to family attitudes, the literature frequently mentions the importance of the attitudes and actions of direct-care staff with respect to the sexual behavior of long-term residents or those in assisted living facilities. Unfortunately, they can sometimes be patronizing, as illustrated by the reaction of one director, a reaction that surprised herself:

> I'll never forget one night I was here. Millie was getting herself ready to go to bed in Mr. Rove's room—and being the mother I am, I said, "You go to your room and he stays in his room." And what right did I have to do this—I just took this stand—"you go to your room"; it sounded like I was talking to my children. . . . He went to bed and . . . I walked her to her room. Didn't say a word to her the whole walk. It was the longest walk I ever took. I said, "Boy, do I have a lot of nerve"—I mean, aren't these two consenting adults?—but I just dismissed them like they were children.[7]

Here we have an echo of our earlier discussion of older adults being regarded as childish and deserving of the treatment that goes with it when it comes to their sexuality. Other subjective judgments by staff can be equally stereotypical or condescending. In Frankowski and Clark's study of assisted living facilities, the general finding was that staff regard their residents as sexless and their sexual behavior as unwelcome.[8] It is important to note that in addition to consulting extensive related literature, this study involved thirteen different facilities, including two predominantly African American homes and three with religious affiliation. The scope and relative diversity of this enterprise is a significant point in favor of its value for our understanding of sexual life in long-term care and assisted living facilities.

Policies Are Important

Given the predictable diversity of views among residents and staff about matters of sexual expression in general and sexual expression in the long-term care environment in particular, having a policy on sexual expression for the facility can be not only helpful but even essential. The safety of the residents engaged in sexual activity, the residents' capacity to consent to sexual activity, the appropriateness of sexual expression given the sensibilities of all residents, the facilitation of privacy, and the interference by family or guardians are all concerns that can be addressed by a thoroughgoing policy on sexual expression.

The Iowa Office of the State Long-Term Care Ombudsman has published *Sexual Expression Policy Development: A Guide for Long-Term Faculties & Assisted Living Programs.* The publication begins by acknowledging that residents of long-term care facilities and assisted living programs are afforded certain rights by federal law, "many of which are relevant to sexuality. These rights include, but are not limited to, the right to privacy, confidentiality, dignity and respect; the right to make independent choices; and the right to choose visitors and meet them in a private location."[9]

A publication of the Health Facilities Division of the Colorado Department of Public Health and Environment (revised September 2004) is even more explicit: "Residents have the right to engage in mutually consenting relationships, regardless of their marital status or sexual orientation. In the community, individuals have the right to engage in extramarital relationships, in spite of any existing religious, moral, or societal norms. There should be no distinction in a long term care facility, provided both residents consent to the relationship."[10] Accordingly, staff have no right to interfere.

The Iowa guidelines provide a seven-step program of policy development that begins with identifying the stakeholders, which would certainly include residents. The list of other potentially relevant participants is a testimony to the complexity of the process: family members, physicians, ethicists, pastoral care workers, long-term care ombudsmen, nurses, therapists, social workers, environmental services workers, and board members.

Following an extensive program of stakeholder education, consulting the literature and other resources, the development of policy guidelines goes forward first with regard to federal and state legal standards. Among other things, the policy should reflect the organization's philosophy, values, and mission statement and determine whether existing policies or rules impede or prevent residents from exercising their right to be sexually expressive. Assessing the facility environment is the next critical step. This is done to gain an understanding of how residents and staff perceive sexuality and the ways that the physical conditions of the facility support or prevent sexual expression. For example, are there physical arrangements that make sexual intimacy possible? Are residents offered access to sexual content in magazines, videos, the internet, and so on? Issues of cognitive capacity to consent also need to be addressed in the policy. (We will look at this prominent concern for long-term care in greater detail later in this chapter.) The final steps of implementation and assessment involve sharing and explaining the policy among all the stakeholders and providing for periodic evaluation.

The Iowa guidelines ask the organization to consider its views on same-sex relationships as it develops its policy. The Colorado publication referred to above is clear that same-sex relationships enjoy the same privileges and privacy rights as heterosexual relationships. The Iowa guidelines ask if the facility provides private physical space for intimacy. The Colorado document maintains that facilities are obligated to make such room available.

The Board of Aging and Long-Term Care—Ombudsman Program for the State of Wisconsin has published *Recommendations for Addressing Resident Relationships*. While the recommendations for policy development are just that—recommendations and not mandates—the policy objective is a consistent reflection of what are generally assumed to be residents' rights:

> The purpose of a resident relationships policy is to affirm and respect the rights of all residents to engage in consensual relationships, whether professional, platonic, married, non-married, intimate or sexual in nature. The policy should uphold the belief that healthy consensual relationships are central to quality of life, and promote an environment that allows individuality, autonomy, dignity and respect to thrive. A facility should welcome and respect all residents, whether lesbian, gay, bisexual, transgendered or heterosexual. A policy should address the right of the resident to engage in any consensual relationship even if the relationship creates challenges to religious, doctrinal, family or societal beliefs, including pertinent privacy and confidentiality issues. At the same time, a facility should acknowledge its responsibility to protect residents who may not be able to consent to sexual relationships. *A policy provides guidance to the multi-disciplinary care team to carry out this balance of rights and protection in all relationships.*[11]

Administrators or ombudsmen, for example, may find the facility's sexual expression policy helpful should the wishes of the family or a guardian be in conflict with the resident's desire and right to be engaged in a consensual sexual relationship that is not impeded by issues of competency to consent. Staff will also be better prepared emotionally and professionally for their encounters with sexual expression among the residents.

River Spring Health: The Hebrew Home at Riverdale

In the literature on sexual expression policy in long-term care, *Policies and Procedures concerning Sexual Expression at the Hebrew Home at Riverdale* is frequently mentioned as an outstanding example.[12] The Hebrew Home in Riverdale, New York, has had a policy on sexual expression since 1995, with the latest revision published in 2013. The document begins with the belief that the older adults residing at the Home have the right to engage in sexual activity as long as they are capable of true consent. It assumes that the civil and privacy rights of all people are also those of the Home's residents. Professional and caregiver staff should set aside their personal biases and uphold this right. The policy provisions then give specific voice to those foundational convictions.

Pursuant to the rights and responsibilities laid out in the policy regarding sexual expression, *sexual expression* is defined as "words, gestures, movements or activities (including pursuing, touching or reading) which appear motivated by a desire for sexual gratification." Unless an act is nonconsensual, involves a minor, poses a risk of sexually transmitted disease (STD) transmission, or represents a public display that is disturbing to the community, residents have the right to sexual expression as defined above.

These rights include legal sexual relations with visitors, access to legal sexually explicit materials (books, magazines, videos, etc.), private space for sexual expression (as possible), and access to professional counseling on sexual matters for self or others. The staff is responsible for upholding these residents' rights to sexual expression. The organization, Hebrew Home, also has responsibilities:

1. The facility should ensure residents' privacy rights and, to the extent possible, make arrangements which facilitate sexual expression, e.g., a private room for one member of a couple.

2. The facility should develop and maintain an orientation and sensitization training program, in order to equip all staff with the skills necessary to upholding the sexual rights of all residents.

3. Through administrative directive and clinical supervision, the facility should ensure that the procedures outlined in this policy, are communicated to and followed by all staff.

The Hebrew Home wants its residents to feel like the facility is their home, where they can pursue their desires as they would in the homes they left. The training programs for staff and the policy itself are designed to engender this experience as much as possible. There is an overriding belief that intimacy is important to the quality of life among residents.[13]

Brethren Hillcrest Homes

Brethren Hillcrest Homes in La Verne, California, is another example of a faith-based organization that has come to understand the need to accommodate expressions of sexual interest and intimacy among its residents. In addition to the question of whether to provide access to and opportunities for intimacy and train staff for this purpose, Hillcrest also addressed questions that have traditionally been matters of moral concern for some of their denominational constituency and that of other Christian communities. Should erotica be tolerated or even provided in living quarters? What about sexual expression between unmarried couples and gay/lesbian coupling? Should condoms be provided to protect against STDs? How do we feel about masturbation? The policy that emerged from the discussion of these and other questions is entitled "Intimate Expression at Hillcrest." It was adopted by the board of directors in 2008.[14]

The policy statements make clear that all residents have the right to privacy for intimate expression that is consensual and free from harmful or abusive behavior. Residents also have a right to access or obtain sexually explicit material and to seek professional consultation pertaining to sexual expression. The staff and the organization are responsible for facilitating the provisions. Under this plan, residents are assured of a nondiscriminatory approach consistent with the Hillcrest admissions practices typical of many such institutions: "Eligible applicants will be considered without regard to gender, race, religion, color, national origin, sexual orientation, political beliefs, disability or ancestry."[15]

Residents' Rights and Questions of Theological Ethics

The overwhelming majority of long-term care communities are religiously affiliated. It is important, therefore, to sample some representative religious approaches to policy and practice regarding sexual expression. Both the Hebrew Home and the Brethren Hillcrest Homes are religiously affiliated institutions, some of whose constituents may well have reservations about the morality of certain forms of sexual expression permitted and facilitated in their institutions. Jewish sexual ethics, which touch on a number of aspects of sexual expression permitted in the Hebrew Home, range along a continuum from very conservative to more liberal.[16] The challenges for Hillcrest are evident in the questions they had to ask of their tradition about the acceptability of specific acts of sexual expression and the institution's role in enabling them.

Chaplains I interviewed in two Lutheran-affiliated homes in Pennsylvania and one in Wisconsin told me that despite not having a written policy, their practice is in accord with the sorts of rights we see afforded to those in the Hebrew Home and Hillcrest. Rights to privacy for sexual expression are honored, and wherever possible, private space is made available for couples, married or not, to share intimate time together. There is no discrimination against LGBTQ persons. Staff in these homes are trained to observe the resident's rights even if they may be personally uncomfortable with some of the activities. However, certainly within the Evangelical Lutheran Church in America (ELCA) membership and leadership, there are a variety of views on the morality of various forms of sexual expression permitted in affiliated long-term care facilities. For example, despite a broad acceptance of sexual diversity in the church, all congregants and congregations are still not comfortable with anything other than heterosexual relations, preferably in the context of marriage. Also the measure of ambiguity in the ELCA social statement *Human Sexuality: Gift and Trust* on cohabitation, which we discussed in the previous chapter, could conceivably shape its outlook on relationships in long-term care facilities despite the deference to residents' rights in its affiliated institutions.

While moral reservations among members of affiliated religious bodies may be inferred from general experience with their traditions, at least one spokesperson for the Roman Catholic Church has made his ethical concerns clear. Father Charles Bourchard's article "Sex and Senior Living: Ethical Questions for Catholic Housing and Long-Term Care" probes the ethical challenge of balancing residents' rights and church teaching. He poses three questions related to senior living facilities, whether independent, assisted living, or skilled nursing:

> First, Is a Catholic senior living facility *cooperating illicitly* in immoral activity if a) it allows physical or sexual intimacy among assisted living

> or nursing home residents who are not married; b) it admits as residents unmarried couples who wish to share an apartment; c) it admits divorced and remarried couples whose previous marriage has not been annulled, or; d) it admits couples that have entered into a civil same-sex marriage? Second, are we requiring inappropriate cooperation of associates, if we ask them to assist patients with certain needs related to sexual intimacy; and third, do we *cause scandal* by admitting couples who will engage in such activities even if there is no significant moral cooperation.[17]

It is clear that the cohabitation of unmarried residents is outside the boundaries of Catholic moral teaching. So also is the case of a couple who have been divorced but at least one of them has not received an annulment. A same-sex couple who has been legally married cannot be considered truly married in the church due to its rejection of same-sex unions as morally illicit. The overriding ethical questions for the institution and its concern for the consciences of staff members is whether they are *cooperating* in morally illicit behavior by serving residents whose sexual conduct is outside the norm and whether the institution may run the risk of *scandal*: "Scandal may be defined as an act, behavior, attitude, or even proximity to evil that leads others to do evil, causes confusion, or weakens their faith."[18]

Father Bourchard is aware of the ageism that the elderly endure and the vulnerability of many seniors. He certainly wants to see Catholic homes as welcoming and caring places where companionship is an antidote to loneliness. While he admits that the article is likely to lead to more questions than answers, he also concludes, "We should encourage companionship and friendship for senior residents. But Catholic institutions cannot ignore our tradition on sexual morality and the virtue of chastity."[19]

In the final analysis, faith-based institutions have to follow the law with respect to residents' rights, notwithstanding any conflict with their tradition's norms of sexual ethics. The law cannot adjudicate morality. Therefore, respect for autonomy and its corollary rights to privacy and free and informed consent cannot be limited except by carefully and professionally discerned evidence of cognitive incapacity for free consent, threat of abuse, or risk of harm.

Respect for individual autonomy, the freedom to make choices and take responsibility for those choices, is a cornerstone of human dignity. In our discussion of the image of God in chapter 1, we noted that the unique relationship of human beings with God that is the image of God involves the freedom and responsibility that are indicative of personhood. Therefore, a biblically based ethic would see respect for autonomy as an obligation grounded in the theology of the image of God. Institutions affiliated with biblically based faith traditions can therefore readily affirm the legal protections of autonomy afforded to long-term care residents. These are rights we all share and are extended to those living in institutions in order to ensure that these are truly their *homes* (as much as is possible).

At the same time, the freedom of sexual expression in the contained environments of long-term care facilities highlights the reality that autonomy is not absolute; it can devolve into selfishness, exploitation, and abuse. Therefore, what is legally permitted with regard to autonomy in sexual expression may raise serious questions about sexual ethics for older people in these facilities. All Christian churches that support long-term care homes and offer the allure of a Christian context may not share the same moral concerns that Father Bourchard has raised, but they still need to work out how compliance with the law and the ethics of Christian love live together without being married. This of course means that before we are done with this book, we need to develop and propose a sexual ethic grounded in Christian love.

Meanwhile, we also need to recognize that autonomy is not absolute given the limits of human finitude. To this end, we now turn to discussions of consent capacity and transmission of STDs, which have their own particular ethical challenges.

Special Concerns

Sexual Consent Capacity

In every written discussion of sexual expression in long-term care that I have studied and in every conversation with persons involved in long-term care, the issue of residents' cognitive capacity to consent to sexual activity is high on the list of concerns. First, persons with some form of cognitive impairment or dementia are not asexual; they do engage in sexual activity.

For the staff in long-term care facilities, this presents a complex ethical challenge. It is recognized, on the one hand, that cognitive impairment or dementia do not necessarily preclude the capacity to consent to sexual activity; on the other hand, they may well diminish or nullify that capacity and open persons to abuse. How, then, can staff honor the residents' rights to autonomy and privacy and yet fulfill the institution's duty to protect residents from harm?

The policy on sexual expression at the Hebrew Home, like all long-term care facilities, recognizes that consent is essential to the right to engage in sexual activity. It supports those who are able to show intact decision-making by words or nonverbal communication, though in some cases, an assessment of that capacity may be indicated. For persons with Alzheimer's disease, a clinical assessment is required using the Home's guidelines, "Assessing Consent to Sexual Activity in Older Adults."[20] Consistent with the approach of the "resident-centered care" movement, the guidelines are focused on asking the resident the following questions and then posing considerations for the professional staff to take into account:

1. Ability to express choices/consent

Ask:

- What are your wishes about this relationship?
- Does your sexual partner make you happy?
- Do you enjoy sexual contact?

Consider:

- Observations and non-verbal clues when older adult is unable to verbalize choices (facial expressions and body language)
- Emotion and mood, before and after sexual contact

2. Ability to appreciate sexual activity

Ask:

- Do you know what it means to have sex?
- What does it mean to you/your partner?

- What would you do if you wanted it to stop?
- What if your partner wanted it to stop?

Consider:

- Nature of the relationship (monogamous)
- Emotion and mood, before and after sexual contact

3. Personal quality of life choices in the here and now

Ask:

- Was and is intimacy important in your life?
- What are your social and companionship needs?
- What brings happiness or fulfillment to your day?

Consider:

- Past and present relationships (including family)
- Impact of cognitive impairment (not an automatic reason to deny relationship)
- Privacy and intimacy rights
- Responsibility to uphold older adults' choices
- Policies for staff education and practice
- Impact of third-party objectives or values on assessment process

Dr. Peter Lichtenberg with his colleague Deborah Strzepek developed an assessment tool in 1990 that remains a mainstay of those working in the field. Writing more recently, Lichtenberg spells out those factors involved in determining capacity to make free choices when a mental health or cognitive disorder is present. First of all, the burden of proof is on those who would deny the ability to consent. Furthermore, that capability relates to the specific decision under consideration, not judgments on overall competence. The older adult must be able to communicate choice, an understanding of the choice, the appreciation of potential consequences of the choice, and the reasoning and rationale for the choice.[21]

The assessment tool is designed to elicit answers to the following questions:

> Does the older adult know who the sexual partner is, and can the older adult accurately state the relationship status, or does the older adult perceive the partner as a spouse? Can the older adult communicate who is initiating the sexual contact, and state the level of intimacy in which they are comfortable? Can the older adult communicate knowledge about the relationship and what the older adult likes or dislikes about the relationship? Can the older adult communicate what he or she wants from the relationship at this time, and how comfortable he or she is with those wants? Finally, and especially for women who have dementia, can the older adult set limits on how sexual the physical intimacy becomes if they want to? How confident is the older person that she would be able to say "no" to unwanted sexual advances and have her wishes respected? Finally, is the person aware of the risks involved in forming the relationship? That is, given the often transitory nature of life in long-term care, what will be the emotional impact should separation occur?[22]

Jennifer Hillman emphasizes the need for an interdisciplinary team approach to assessment. The team should include psychologists, physicians (geriatricians and psychiatrists), social workers, occupational and physical therapists, nurses, nurse's assistants, and legal guardians, family members, and ombudsmen as appropriate. With respect to family members, resident approval may be needed for their participation. She then offers an extensive description of an interview process designed to assess the three primary criteria for the capacity to consent: knowledge, reasoning, and voluntariness.[23]

Dr. Eran Metzger, writing in the *AMA Journal of Ethics*, provides a case study that illustrates the sort of ethical deliberation that can arise when a person's cognitive capacity for consent to sexual activity is in question:

> One afternoon, Drs. Brian and Anderson receive a consultation request regarding Mrs. Shera, an 80-year-old woman living in the nursing home section who has dementia. When reviewing her record, Dr. Brian sees that she was admitted to the long-term care facility about six months ago after living independently with her husband of 55 years. Over time, it became more difficult for him to manage some of her behavioral issues at home. For instance, when she would take walks through the woods near their

> house, she would get lost on the paths. Sometimes, the police were called to search for her and take her home. When Mr. Shera tried to limit her excursions, she would become severely irritable, yelling at him and ultimately swinging at him when he tried to keep her from leaving the house. These episodes would last about 5–10 minutes, at which point Mrs. Shera would shut down and then forget what had just happened.
>
> In the nursing home, Mr. Shera visited her as much as he could and she was always happy to see him. Once, a nurse walked into Mrs. Shera's room and found her and her husband in bed together with some of their clothes removed. After Mr. Shera left, the nurse returned to talk further with Mrs. Shera about what had happened. Mrs. Shera indicated that she loved her husband and that he was a good man, but she wasn't able to answer questions about whether she felt comfortable engaging sexually with him. Troubled that Mrs. Shera's illness compromises her decision-making capacity, the nurse discussed her concerns with Drs. Brian and Anderson. After talking with Mrs. Shera, the nurse and the two physicians still were not clear whether and how it was appropriate for Mr. Shera to engage sexually with Mrs. Shera. They wondered what to do.[24]

Using the criteria developed by Lichtenberg and Strzepek, discussed above and echoed by Hillman, the two psychiatrists will attempt to determine the extent to which Mrs. Shera understands the situation and how willing she is to participate. Mr. Shera could possibly be enlisted to assess what is going on. How sensitive is he to his wife's needs and desires? What kind of sexual activity does he intend and is it consistent with their sexual history together? Can he speak to his awareness and sensitivity to fact that her desires may change from day to day? Can he give assurance that he will be protective of her safety? Whatever the outcome in this case, Metzger points out that a diagnosis of dementia is not prima facie evidence of a lack of capacity to consent. Just because one can't manage one's finances, for example, does not mean they can't consent to sexual activity.[25]

While Mr. Shera certainly has a stake in this situation, the one under the care of the nursing home and the one most vulnerable is Mrs. Shera. The staff's interest in protecting her from harm is in a delicate balance with her rights to privacy and a sexual relationship. Does ethical reasoning conclude that only a sure verdict of incapacity or evidence of abuse on the husband's part would meet the burden of proof required to restrict her sexual relationship with him? It would seem so, but how certain can they be that the burden of proof has been met in this case? Much of ethical decision-making is a matter of discernment in complex circumstances. We have guidelines, but they do not provide the answers in and of themselves. Given what can be learned and discerned from the various dimensions of this situation, can staff conclude that they are not failing in their duty to prevent harm should they give their blessing to the couple's ongoing relationship?

Lichtenberg sharpens the ethical issue for us by contrasting two approaches taken by nursing homes he has worked in. The prosexuality position prioritizes autonomy and a belief in the physical and emotional health benefits of ongoing sexual expression. However, there are hazards to this approach, as illustrated by a case he cites: A cognitively impaired male initiated a sexual relationship with a more cognitively impaired female. The staff allowed it to go on, saying they had a "special relationship," only to find out that the woman agreed because she mistakenly thought he was her husband.[26]

What Lichtenberg calls the antisexuality position is typified by administrations that prioritize avoiding exploitation, abuse, transmission of STDs, and violation of modesty values older folks are presumed to have. As a result, a serious assessment of capacity may be rare, and assumptions of incapacity are often based simply on the existence of a guardian or on poor communications skills. These untested assumptions, coupled with a legitimate fear of openness to investigation for abuse should sexual activity be allowed, combine to deprive residents who may have the capacity to consent to sexual relations.[27]

Ethically responsible discernment requires that we ask, "What is going on?" That is a question we ask of the dynamic of the situation and the relevant facts to the extent that we can determine them. But it is also a question we ask of ourselves. What feelings do I have about this? What are my motives? Do I have biases that are affecting my discernment and possibly my decision? In both the prosexuality and the antisexuality cases Lichtenberg describes, those questions aren't being pursued. Both in terms of seeking the facts by an assessment of capacity and in terms of failing to consider their respective biases, the staff and administration have not sought to know what's going on. In the latter case, there are also the conflicting claims of residents' rights versus institutional liability. However, before entering into a resolution-of-conflict process, one must first know what's going on. Maybe there really isn't a conflict.

Sexually Transmitted Diseases

There is no question that with the increase of sexual activity among older adults (recognized or not), there has been an increase in STDs, especially HIV/AIDS. Other STDs have also been on the increase in this older age group, including chlamydia, syphilis, gonorrhea, and sometimes sexually transmitted hepatitis C.[28] Although this discussion is placed here in the chapter on long-term care, it is a concern that extends beyond such residential facilities to senior living out in the community. An article from HuffPost accounts for this development in a rather colorful way:

> The high-level answer [for this increase in STDs] is older men take potent little pills to help with erectile dysfunction coupled with (pun intended) post-menopausal older women, with no pregnancy concerns, using progesterone and estrogen creams that help arouse them and makes sex more enjoyable for them. This combination of factors adds up to a whole lot of unprotected sex. In fact, what goes on in nursing homes, assisted living facilities, or other large residential congregations of elderly people is a lot closer to what goes on in spring break hotels than most people would ever imagine. With lots of sex comes the possibilities of lots of STDs. The reality is your college-aged daughter on spring break and your grandmother in the nursing home should each be equally worried about catching chlamydia from the guy (or the grandfather) next door.[29]

The use of drugs to deal with erectile dysfunction has made sexual intercourse more likely among older adults and, without the fear of pregnancy, for postmenopausal women. Condom use is also less likely. In part as a consequence of assumptions about the asexuality of older people, older adults have not been the focus of safe-sex campaigns, including the knowledge that oral sex is not inherently "safe sex." Also, health care providers are much less likely to speak of HIV/AIDS risks with their older patients. Drugs and alcohol, more frequently involved among older adults than some might expect, can contribute to risky sexual behaviors.[30] The increased use of online dating by seniors involves the risk of engagement with partners whose sexual history is unknown. As people age, their immune systems weaken, making them more susceptible to STDs.[31]

Robert Youdin shares this true story of a man he calls Marvin. The vignette is entitled "Having the Best Time of My Life."[32] Marvin was an eighty-six-year-old retiree living in a Florida retirement community. Though faithful to his wife of fifty-two years, he found their sex life boring and unexciting. After she died, he found himself in a community in which women greatly outnumbered the men. The mean age of the residents was eighty-one.

Marvin discovered to his surprise that the women there were being flirtatious with him. Marvin started to fantasize about these women until finally, he decided it was time to date for the first time since his wife's death. Marvin made a date with a woman Youdin calls Linda, who seemed the kind who might make a good mate. Again, to his surprise, Linda suggested that they "fool around," and Marvin complied. The next morning after a night of sexual activity, Linda informed him that he was the "talk of the town." With so few men in the community, Linda joked, "If you have a penis and are still breathing, you are hot." Being as he was in good shape, rich, smart, and handsome, Linda said, "You can have any woman here whenever you want." Marvin responded that he was looking for a committed relationship, but Linda said, "Forget about it—women here want to have fun, and besides, how much longer do you think you will live?"

Marvin followed Linda's lead and began dating a number of women and enjoyed multiple sexual encounters. "I'm having the best time of my life," he said. Unfortunately, after a year of this activity, Marvin was diagnosed with HPV (human papillomavirus), one of the most common sexually transmitted infections. His doctor advised him to use a condom and also to warn his sexual partners of his disease so that they could be checked out by their own physicians. He was embarrassed at having to admit to having HPV and unwilling to use a condom. He never had because he felt that with a condom, he couldn't feel anything and, therefore, couldn't maintain an erection. He ceased dating and became depressed and isolated. Eventually, he sought therapy in hopes of returning to his exciting sex life but with "safe sex" practices.

Marvin's story graphically illustrates what studies tell us about the dangers of STDs in the sex lives of older adults. It also raises the moral issue of promiscuity, regardless of the dangers of disease. The "hookup" culture of the younger generation and the practice of "friends with benefits" have their own iterations in the senior context. Even as we affirm the sexuality of the elderly, the question arises as to how the ethical compass of Christian love should direct sexual expression in later life. Youdin and the studies just cited are not interested in that question, but we are. And we shall attend to it before we're done. There are "Marvins" and "Lindas" out there.

Sensitivity to Needs of LGBTQ Persons in Long-Term Care

Our previous discussions have already made us aware of the fact that older LGBTQ persons, like heterosexual adults, continue to have sexual desires and needs for intimacy into old age. Like all other seniors in long-term care communities who are sexually active, they require privacy and respect for their sexuality. However, understanding and appreciating these realities has been a work in progress.

Amber Hollibaugh, an activist on behalf of the LGBTQ community, reports on interviews she conducted some years ago with staff of what she described as "liberal" nursing homes. What she found, among other things, was that the ageist idea of the asexual elderly was conflated with an ignorance of LGBTQ realities, creating the false impression among staff that they had no known LGBTQ residents. Compounding that sort of denial was the fear on the part of residents that if they outed themselves as LGBTQ, they would be shunned and maybe asked to leave. Besides the fear of difference that is a frequent human response, the negative attitudes lurking behind the fears of some staff and residents were born of a perceived close association of LGBTQ sexuality with HIV/AIDS. Fortunately, Hollibaugh concludes that times are changing, and the sexuality and erotic lives of older adults, LGBTQ or heterosexual, are gaining respect and attention.[33]

Building that understanding and respect that Hollibaugh anticipated is in large measure the purpose of Tim R. Johnston's book *Welcoming LGBT Residents: A Practical Guide for Senior Living Staff*. An educated staff trained to understand and respect the sexuality and sexual desires of LGBTQ persons is essential to creating a welcoming and safe home. That the staff understand that they are working in the residents' "home" is important to inculcating that feeling of belonging for all residents. Moreover, the growing number of LGBTQ folks entering long-term care includes many "boomers" who, like their heterosexual counterparts, are more ready to communicate their sexual needs. A well-educated and alert staff is required to meet this emerging population. In our contemporary situation, we see sexual identity to be more fluid and diverse than in the past; just knowing and understanding the language of sexual identity is in itself a helpful step. A review of the history of discrimination and pain along with the successes in greater openness that are integral to the life experiences of elderly members of the LGBTQ community is an essential part of the curriculum for those who would serve these people. Appreciating how many times in their lives LGBTQ elders have had to "come out" for different people and in different contexts and now must come out yet again in this residential context can evoke both compassion and respect on the part of the staff.[34]

Johnston's extensive discussion of steps in making long-term care facilities welcoming for LGBTQ elders goes hand in hand with the organization he works for as a project director: SAGE: Advocacy & Services for LGBT Elders. Together with the Human Rights Campaign Foundation, SAGE offers a program called the Long-Term Care Equality Index (LEI). Its goal is to create a network of long-term care communities across the country that provide welcoming homes for older LGBTQ people:

> Communities that participate in the Long-Term Care Equality Index (LEI) have a tool developed in collaboration with experts nationwide to support their work towards a diverse and inclusive environment for all residents, including LGBTQ older adults. The LEI supports communities by providing access to a confidential self-assessment by which a community

> can measure the degree of its LGBTQ inclusiveness on a range of benchmarks that have been established by national LGBTQ and aging services leaders. Once completed, communities receive specific information about their own strengths and weaknesses, along with targeted guidance rooted in best practices, that describes practical policies and procedures that improve inclusivity for LGBTQ older adults.[35]

Details of how this program works in real life are punctuated with stories of older LGBTQ adults whose residential environment has made them afraid to be open about their sexuality and their relationship with a lover whom they euphemistically call "friend." On the SAGE website, Ruth Long-Higgins, executive director of the Ruth Parker Center for Abundant Aging, United Church Homes, tells the story of this faith-based organization's journey to becoming "open [to] and affirming" of LGBTQ people. The journey includes embracing the SAGECare educational program for long-term care staff development.[36] United Church Homes is a ministry of the United Church of Christ, providing us with another example of inclusive faith-based care. To be open and affirming in this church community is a matter of ethical commitment rooted in the core tenets of the faith, not simply an accommodation to legal requirements.

Of course, when it comes to the lives of LGBTQ people, religion—more often than not, in the past and still in the present—has been painfully unkind. A recent Canadian study bemoaned many of the deficits of care for LGBTQ folks in long-term care communities that Johnston and SAGE are concerned with. The authors added this comment: "Religious teachings against homosexuality and conducive to a heteronormative cultural order have influenced not only lesbian and gay individuals, but also professional counselors, who are called on to work with them. Even when administrators and direct service staff indicate that they are comfortable serving LGBT people and believe in the importance of providing them with affirming, high-quality care, they may also have little knowledge of LGBT-specific health concerns. Few agencies actually implement policies and programs that specifically target LGBT older adults."[37]

Notwithstanding this history of discrimination at the hands of religious bodies, the role of religious faith remains deeply important to members of the LGBTQ community. Therefore, clinicians concerned for the support of these residents should take note of the resources of faith in their approach to care.[38]

In my own experience as director of our ELCA church-wide study of the church and homosexuality, I was deeply impressed by the stalwart faith of members of our church's LGBTQ community. During every session of our task force discussion, they were there to listen respectfully despite the fact that they were submitted to the disturbing evidence of a conflicted church that had not yet decided what to do. They unfailingly offered to meet and talk with individuals and congregations for the sake of greater understanding. Thankfully, the church eventually opened its doors for persons in committed same-sex relationships to serve in its ministries and reiterated its open and affirming stance to all. I like to think that the experience of doing the study in congregations throughout the church combined with the persistent faith of the LGBTQ community had a great deal to do with that outcome.

Part Three

Mapping the Way of Christian Love

Chapter Five

Sexuality, Values, and Vocation

My life is like a frozen thing. No bud nor greenness can I see; Yet rise it shall—the sap of Spring; O Jesus, rise in me.

—Christina Rossetti

No one is too old to begin something new . . . we are always standing at the beginning.

—Jürgen Moltmann

The previous four chapters have sought to be descriptive of sexuality in later life, both its myths and its realities. Ethical issues have been raised, and some responses from the larger Christian community have been recorded. It is time now to move toward a theological and ethical account of human sexuality and how it speaks to the sexual lives of those in later life. While the needs and circumstances of the aged are special in certain respects, they are included in what we say about faith and sexuality for people of all ages and sexual orientations. To do anything else would be a form of ageist disregard for their sexuality. Therefore, we start now to move toward the development of a comprehensive, faith-based perspective on human sexuality that will have implications for all. Within that framework, we can begin to speak specifically to the sexuality and lives of older adults.

To Be Human Is to Be Sexual in the Unity of Body and Spirit

Genesis 1:27 and 2:22–25 tell us that human beings are created as sexual beings. Our sexuality is inherent in the physicality of our creation in the image of God. As we noted in chapter 1, our created relatedness to God is at the core of the image of God, a sign of our spiritual being. In Genesis 2:7, God breathes into the human the breath of life, the *Ruach Yahweh*, the life-giving spirit. We understand ourselves in the divine image as a spiritual-physical unity.[1] In Margaret Farley's adroitly chosen words, we are "embodied spirits" and "inspirited bodies."[2] And when we consider, as we also did in chapter 1, that the *imago Dei* is the *imago Trinitatis*, we understand the essence of our humanity as people created for communion and union with God and one another. Our lives are destined by creation to be a reflection of the unity of the persons of the Trinity in the bonds of love. The unity of Father, Son, and Holy Spirit in the ineffable mystery of the Trinity is a unity of love—so deep and inexpressible that each lives in the other, inseparable. Existence in the image of the Trinity is that we are made by love and for love. This lasts forever. Therefore, in all stages of life, we are lover and beloved. This is true in all relations of life and in and through the expression of our sexuality.

However, under the pressure of teachings about human sin and the "temptations of the flesh," dualistic ideas have compromised the ideal of the physical-spiritual unity of biblical anthropology. These dualistic impulses that elevate the spiritual and cast a cloak of suspicion over the physical have historically had a particularly damaging effect on the theology of human sexuality. We saw this in the seeming ambivalence about sexuality in Paul's comments in 1 Corinthians 7 and in the well-known fear of sexuality and its dangerous possibilities in many of the early church theologians.

We have also had a brief account of how the Reformation broke through that tradition in its refutation of celibacy as the higher and holier way—the way of the spirit versus the way of the flesh. And we know too that the culture and (to a great extent) the churches have gone a long way—some would say way too far—from the fear of sex to an affirmation of sex. Yet for all of that, as flawed human beings, there is still a need for us to seek a unity of body and spirit in our sexual lives if we are to be true to the ideal of our birthright in the image of God.

In the Song of Solomon, or Song of Songs, we have a poetic expression of erotic love, an affirmation of human sexuality and the sexual passion that drives us toward unity with the other in the bonds of love. It is a celebration of erotic pleasure but not in a profane sense of the "erotic" that is associated with the so-called lust of the flesh. Rather, we see here the deep-seated longing of the enfleshed human spirit taken up in aesthetic pleasure at the presence of created beauty, radiantly alive and self-giving. So we have this exchange between the lovers:

> How fair and pleasant you are, O loved one, delectable maiden! You are stately as a palm tree, and your breasts are like its clusters. I say I will climb the palm tree and lay hold of its branches. O may your breasts be like clusters of the vine, and the scent of your breath like apples, and your kisses like the best wine that goes down smoothly, gliding over lips and teeth. I am my beloved's, and his desire is for me. Come, my beloved, let us go forth into the fields, and lodge in the villages; let us go out early to the vineyards, and see whether the vines have budded, whether the grape blossoms have opened and the pomegranates are in bloom. There I will give you my love. (Song of Solomon 7:6–12)

David Carr has reviewed various interpretations of the Song over time. He observes that we have seen spiritual interpretations that deny sexual meaning—not two human lovers but allegorical readings of love between God and Israel or between Christ and the church. However, there have also been sexual readings that deny any spiritual meaning or significance. So he concludes that the spirituality-sexuality dichotomy continues in the history of interpreting the Song.[3]

This dichotomy Carr sees in the interpretations of the Song points us beyond the scholarly debate over the text to a broader reality. Dualistic impulses still exist within contemporary culture and religious thought. For the sexual-only reading of the Song, one can see a parallel in the secularization of contemporary sexuality, devoid of any spiritual referent. We have seen this tendency in the clinical approach to sexual interaction in long-term care communities where the main ethical, not to say legal, principle operative is "do no harm." Though respect will be shown for the spiritual and moral concerns of residents, there is no spiritual dimension to this policy save an underlying humanitarian spirit. Indeed, we should not expect anything else in what is basically a secular context of legally conferred rights that prevails, even for religiously based institutions.

The spiritual-only reading prompts us to reckon with the fact that Christian communities are not entirely at home with liberation from the dualism of the past. Ageist attitudes toward the sexuality of the elderly may well reveal a dismissal of the abiding value of sexual intimacy. The physical reality of diversity in sexual orientation remains a spiritual struggle for many in the wider Christian community. Ironically, the moral/spiritual objection to the sexuality of those who are not heterosexual is based not on any consideration of the spiritual dimension of their sexual lives but rather on the bare *physical* expression of their sexuality—that is, physicality cancels spirituality.

The quest for the unity of body and spirit in our sexual lives remains as the quest to be true to our creation and destiny as image of God. Carr seeks an interpretation of the Song that will put sexuality and spirituality back together rather than interpretations that have argued it is one or the other but not both. Carr is not interested in the resolution of a hermeneutical contest for its own sake. His concern, as ours, is to see in this discussion of the text a stepping-stone to arriving at a foundational insight for a Christian theology and ethics of human sexuality.

Carr offers several ways of thinking about the integral connection of the spiritual and the physical in our sexuality: "Eros is a fundamental spiritual impulse to reach out from ourselves for connection, to become vulnerable, often against other instincts."[4] Vulnerability is at the heart of the self-giving aspect of the neighbor love Jesus commanded and of those expressions of love we associate with eros. That is, we entrust ourselves to the other, place our trust in them, risking in so doing that we will be hurt or rejected. This risk, this entrusting, is sometimes against our instincts of self-protection and the desire to stay in control. The vulnerability of love echoes the dynamics of faith as the ongoing act of entrusting ourselves to the promises of God. Again, as we noted in chapter 1, the tragedy of the primordial myth of the garden of Eden lay in the temptation to control: "You will be like God," said the serpent (Genesis 3:5). We are created by love for love, but a protective, even jealous love of self often stands in the way.

Carr goes on to suggest that we think of erotic connections as a taste of the very best of God's creation—as "powerful signs of God's presence in our lives." However, he says, "the most we experience in life are partial tastes of ultimate fulfillment, brief hints of the greater good for which we long."[5] This eschatological perspective is something I will take up in the next section of this chapter as I bring some of my own work to bear upon this subject. In the meantime, Carr's reflections on the Song have given us a biblical window through which to look at the larger landscape of our lived sexuality—to see it in terms of the intimate connection of the spiritual and physical at the heart of the love that is our creation and destiny.

The View from the Future

We have seen that ageist assumptions about the sexuality of older people are directed at all sexual orientations. The dismissal of their sexuality is at the same time the devaluation of the humanity of the elderly; to be human is to be sexual. People who are heterosexual and people of the LGBTQ community may also share the burden of disapproval by others as they try to live out their sexual lives and seek loving relationships. Notwithstanding our more open-minded culture, unmarried older adults who cohabit or find each other in the long-term care community have the censure of many Christian churches, as we have seen. The LGBTQ community has the censure of major church bodies who regard sexual unions outside the tradition of heteronormativity as against God's will at any age. The Roman Catholic Church, the Southern Baptist churches, and other conservative bodies have made it clear that anything other than legal marriage between a man and a woman will not receive the blessing of the church. Even mainline churches that have been open and affirming of all sexual orientations still have individual members and even entire congregations that cannot subscribe to that view.

I think meeting the theological challenge of heterosexism is a good starting point for the development of an inclusive theology of human sexuality that also speaks to sexual life in old age and the important theme of vocation that I introduced in chapter 1.[6] I'll start with the issue of same-sex unions or same-sex marriage as the entry point.

Same-Sex Unions and the Order of Creation

Anyone who has had any experience of the debate in the churches over the moral status of same-sex unions is familiar with the appeals to specific texts believed to condemn all same-sex sexual activity.[7] For many, this settles the matter; same-sex lovemaking is sinful. The legalization of same-sex marriage has not changed the views of those who hold to this position. For others, these texts are not that clear in all cases, are culturally conditioned, and are ignorant of our modern understanding of sexual orientation. Thus, many would argue, the morality of same-sex love should be judged instead by the same values of fidelity, justice, and self-giving love traditionally associated with heterosexual unions.

Even if those who take a dim view of gay and lesbian sexual relations concede some plausibility to the cultural gap between the prohibitive texts and present understanding, they can still appeal to the "order of creation." Though *order of creation* is not itself a biblical term, it is believed to fit the fact that the biblical theology of creation in regard to sexuality is clearly heterosexual in design. The union of a man and a woman in what we have come to call marriage is the norm for sexual union. From this, the argument follows that the entire range of sexual orientations we name as LGBTQ are disordered phenomena of a fallen world. Consequently, it is maintained, same-sex unions, for example, are morally unacceptable regardless of the faithful, loving, and just qualities they may embody. This conclusion is thought to both give credence to and find support from the disputed texts that condemn certain same-sex acts.[8]

Marriage as an Order of Creation: The Tradition and Its Defenders

The foundations of heterosexual marriage as an order of creation to the exclusion of all other forms of sexual union were certainly laid before the time of the Reformation. However, the notion of "orders of creation" was a distinctive contribution of Luther's doctrine of God's twofold reign and his teaching on vocation. According to Luther, the principal orders that God has providentially established are ministry, marriage, and government. Within these orders are many forms of leadership and service, including parenthood, economic stewardship, and a host of government positions and functions. For Luther, marriage as an institution, along with the other orders and their various expressions, stands under the civil use of God's law and is a matter for the civil authorities. Accordingly, he saw marriage as a way to protect people and society from the destructive potential of unbridled sexual activity. At the same time, and more importantly for our immediate purposes, Luther also saw marriage between a man and a woman as God's original intention for creation prior to the fall.[9] So Luther extols the glory and gravity of marriage as God's premier creation: "He [God] has established it before all others as the first of all institutions, and he created man and woman differently (as is evident) not for indecency but to be true to each other, to be fruitful, to beget children, and to nurture and bring them up to the glory of God."[10]

Marriage as an order of creation includes the blessing of procreation and the vocation of parenthood. However, Luther did not see procreation as the sole purpose of legitimating sex in marriage, as some of the ancients did. One senses in his writings a deep appreciation for the loving companionship that marriage affords, which is a fundamental blessing and purpose of marriage. We might also note that Luther's desire to extol marriage as God's plan was an integral part of his attack on the church's elevation of celibacy. I would like to suggest that attitudes that dismiss and even denounce sexual activity in later life are a de facto return to support for celibacy as the morally superior choice for the elderly, as it once was considered for those in holy orders.

Historically and theologically, the idea of the order of creation regarding sexuality is a sibling to one form of natural law argument: we can discern

God's will by what the Creator has revealed in nature. This doctrine has been associated with the Roman Catholic tradition and its rejection of same-sex relations as unnatural. However, we have heard recent Protestant voices saying much the same thing. The late Princeton theologian and ethicist Max Stackhouse asserted that "homosexuality is contrary to the intentions of creation. The structure of sex organs is such that one of their purposes is human reproduction . . . and it is a purpose not capable of being fulfilled homosexually."[11]

The normative import of the heterosexual design of God's creation is also a major theme in biblical scholar Robert Gagnon's argument against same-sex sexual relations. The created anatomy of male and female, he argues, makes them "perfect fits" for one another, in contrast to male-male or female-female unions. He continues, "Hence, already at the start of the canon, in the description of human origins in Genesis 1–3, a justification for male-female union is provided: the physical, interpersonal, and procreative sexual complementarity of male and female. As we shall see, this motif will reappear as a continuous thread in the Old Testament, early Jewish and New Testament critiques of same-sex intercourse as 'contrary to nature.'"[12]

The Challenge

Marriage as an order of creation and related arguments from nature or natural law have proven to be durable keystones of the case against the acceptance of same-sex sexual relations and the ecclesiastical blessing of such unions. Moreover, as noted earlier, they have often been invoked to give credence and force to condemnatory biblical texts of otherwise disputed meaning and relevance. As we have noted, although much progress has been made in the acceptance of LGBTQ sexuality, and same-sex marriage is now legal, the Christian community worldwide is still divided over the acceptability of any sexual relationship other than heterosexual marriage. Those who are not open and affirming of sexual diversity have also made their views heard in the public sector as they press for exemptions from antidiscrimination laws. Given this state of affairs, it seems clear for those of us who bemoan the discrimination within the churches against LGBTQ people that an alternative account is needed. That is, the Christian community needs a cogent, biblically based theology of human sexuality that is affirming of sexual diversity—one that goes beyond debating single texts or making a general appeal to neighbor love. This task will require challenging the orders of creation tradition.

Important as it is, more is at stake than the question of the moral status of same-sex unions or sexual expression among LGBTQ people. Speaking to their situation will lead us to speak of sexuality in general. I believe what I now propose in the reframing of the orders of creation tradition is significant for a more comprehensive theology and ethics of human sexuality.

Helmut Thielicke and the "Orders"

A first step toward my goal is a brief dialogue with the prominent twentieth-century German theologian Helmut Thielicke. His views on the orders of creation in general and on marriage and sexuality in particular offer a transition from the perspective of the past to the perspective of the future.

What Thielicke refers to as the "orders of history"—the law, the state, the economic order, and other structures of authority in the organization of human affairs—have been understood in the past to be orders of creation; however, Thielicke rejects that designation for these structures. They belong, he says, to the world of fallen humanity; they cannot be described as *created*, for that would suggest that they are good by nature. As such, these orders are best thought of as "orders of divine patience" or "emergency orders" designed to preserve us from ourselves, including the necessity of curbing violence with violence.[13] The orders of social and political structures change with the events of history and can therefore also be called "orders of history." This is already an important step in reframing the idea of orders, one that many theologians followed after him.

However, for Thielicke, there is one order that *is* an order of creation. He believes that marriage, the union of a man and woman, is a true order of creation established by God before the fall: "In its original intention its status [marriage] was to be that of a partnership between man and woman

(Gen 2:18), a state of being created for each other (2:21–22) and of recognizing themselves in each other (2:23)."[14] At the same time, he recognizes that the patterns of marriage have changed throughout history and from culture to culture. Thus no particular form of marriage is an order of creation per se. What is primordial is "the interfusion of eros and agape"[15] (the neighbor love Jesus commanded) in a monogamous relationship between a man and a woman. In this blend of eros and agape, the conduct and values we associate with agape, such as fidelity and mutuality and deep caring, form the core of what makes for a morally healthy union in whatever public form it may take.

Unlike the other major theologians who were his contemporaries, Thielicke was sympathetic to the trials faced by gay and lesbian couples of his day. For him, their relations were not an ethical problem; they could live in responsible partnerships according to the same values as we expect in a traditional marriage. Nonetheless, their relationship in view of the primordial order of creation is "disordered" and cannot be completely affirmed. In sum, gay and lesbian couples living by the norms of marital love can achieve a "relative ethical order" even though, theologically speaking, their reality is contrary to the order of creation.[16]

Thielicke is an important transitional figure between past views of human sexuality and new ways of thinking. He does hold to the belief that the union of male and female in what he calls the "interfusion of eros and agape" in a monogamous commitment consistent with agape love is God's plan for creation. However, this primordial order is not tied to any specific historical expression of marriage. This in itself invites a dialogue about contemporary views of marriage. So, for example, does the interfusion of eros and agape in the committed relationship of a cohabiting elderly couple qualify as a morally valid union, a marriage in the sight of God? Before gay and lesbian couples had the option of legal marriage, some in the churches argued that their loving commitment should be blessed as "marriage in the sight of God."[17]

Thielicke's idea of sexual union as the interfusion of eros and agape is also a link to the sort of sexual ethic implicit in Carr's vision of the unity of spiritual and physical. There is no hint here of the sort of spiritual-physical dualism that underlaid the repression of sexuality in the past and has come to separate sexuality from spirituality for so many in the present.

Finally, the values of a truly loving marriage are not outside the possibility of couples who are not heterosexual. No one is excluded from the possibility of a loving and just sexual partnership. The real problem is a theological one: the heterosexual order of creation. Let's challenge that doctrine from the perspective of the future. At first this argument will apply mainly to the concerns of the LGBTQ community, but it will soon spread out to encompass the concerns of all, including the elderly.

Eschatology, Anthropology, and Sexuality

In Dietrich Bonhoeffer's *Creation and Fall: A Theological Exposition of Genesis 1–3*, he has this to say concerning the image of God: "The attempt—with the origin and nature of humankind in mind—to take a gigantic leap back into the world of the lost beginning, to seek to know for ourselves what humankind was like in its original state and to identify our own ideal of humanity with what God actually created is hopeless. It fails to recognize that it is only from the Christ that we can know about the original nature of humankind. . . . Only in the middle, as those who live from Christ, do we know about the beginning."[18]

Bonhoeffer's definition of our reality as penultimate places the meaning and direction of our lives under the sway of the ultimate. As such, he provides us with a highly suggestive antecedent to the eschatological theologies that were to follow the likes of Wolfhart Pannenberg and Jürgen Moltmann.[19]

The Image of God as Eschatological Destiny

First Corinthians 15:42–58 tells us that the fulfillment of humanity's creation in the image of God is a promise of the resurrection. It is thus an eschatological promise at the arrival of God's reign, consistent with the future-oriented trajectory of the Bible and particularly Jesus's proclamation of the coming reign of God and his self-understanding as the one who was bringing it in. Indeed, Jesus's resurrection against the backdrop of expectation for the resurrection of the dead at the arrival of God's eschatological reign was, Pannenberg has famously argued, the appearance of that ultimate future in our history.[20] This understanding is at the heart of Pannenberg's conviction that the Bible is future oriented and that, despite biblical sources positing an original perfection, Christians need not insist on that notion. Rather, Paul's testimony in 1 Corinthians 15:45–49 points to the fulfillment of creation as eschatological.[21]

Jürgen Moltmann seems a bit more straightforward in clearly rejecting the idea of a perfect paradise state shattered by the fall. Instead, he offers an eschatological view of creation in which the culmination of creation is the arrival of something entirely new.[22]

Ted Peters spells out the implications of Pannenberg's and Moltmann's thoughts when he asserts that God creates from the future, not the past: "God creates continually and will not finish this creative work until the creation is consummated in the eschaton. The destiny of all things determines what they are."[23]

Biblical scholar Terrence Fretheim sees God's creating action in the Bible as threefold: originating creation, continuing creation, and completing creation.[24] Completing creation is God's eschatological action that brings a new heaven and earth into being: "The books of Genesis and Revelation provide a creational bracket for the Bible, and texts in between are a continuing witness to the purposive work of God toward this new creation. At the same time, the new creation is not a return to the original beginning."[25]

This futurist theological perspective grounded in the biblical symbol of the reign of God is the frame in which we place our further consideration of anthropology under the symbol of the image of God. The idea that the fulfillment of our humanity in the divine image is a matter of destiny has a history in Christian thought. Irenaeus, the great second-century theologian, thought of the first human being at the beginning of creation as a child destined to grow but not yet complete:

> It is the distinctive characteristic of a child that he grows and becomes . . . man is created in the *imago* and *similitudo* of God, but he is not God's *imago* and *similitudo*—only the eternal Son is that, and only he possesses

> the whole of God's fullness in himself. Man is created for the Son, and he attains his perfection in the Son. His destiny was realized only when the image of God took human life in the Incarnation and took up into himself the man who had been created in the image of God. The Incarnation and its benefits had no reality when man was first created: man, therefore, is a child, son, whose goal and objective is full growth.[26]

For Irenaeus, humanity's growth toward fulfillment is God's creating activity. Not until Augustine (354–430 CE) do we see a theology of original perfection that is so important for the establishment of the order of creation concept.

If, then, we can say that our existence in the image of God, our authentic humanity, resides in the promise of God's future—the arrival of the new creation (2 Corinthians 5:17), the realization of a new heaven and a new earth (Revelation 21:1)—we should follow Bonhoeffer and look to the Christ who we have seen is the revealer of that future.

Christ is "the image of the invisible God" (Colossians 1:15–20). The journey to our destiny in the divine image, humanity's participation in the completion of creation, is one of being transformed according to his image by the work of the Spirit (2 Corinthians 3:18). These two passages alone alert us to the insight that creation, redemption, and sanctification coalesce as the unified act of the Trinity in the fulfillment of creation at the arrival of God's future. The focus for our understanding of what the image truly means is our becoming in Christ, in whose image we are being transformed. In him, our destiny is for that communion and union with God and each other in the bonds of love that he preached and embodied in the perfect unity of human and divine in his own being.

Further steps are now needed to develop the theological foundations of an inclusive sexual ethic. What more can we say about human fulfillment in the coming reign of God, and how does it bear upon our sexual ethics in the present? We take up the first part of this question presently and the second part in the final section.

Trinity, Community, and Sexuality

As already observed, we are being transformed according to the image of God as revealed in the Christ. The Christ is the revelation of our destiny for the fulfillment of community with God and one another in the bonds of love. This community is analogous to the community of love in the unity of the Trinity and of the divine and human in Christ. Again, the *imago Dei* is the *imago Trinitatis.* So I want to build now on the earlier discussions of the Trinity.

Contemporary theologies of the Trinity are rich and involved, deserving of more space than I can give in this context. Suffice it to say that contemporary thinkers such as Jürgen Moltmann, Catherine Mowry LaCugna, Leonardo Boff, and John Zizioulas have emphasized relationality and community as the essence of Trinitarian unity. The unity of the Trinity is centered on the construct of *perichoresis*, or the mutual indwelling of the persons of the Trinity with one another in the bonds of love. The love revealed for the world by the Christ is the very self-giving love that constitutes the divine life of the Trinity.

Stanley Grenz was attuned to this theological discourse. He concluded therefore that the eschatological fulfillment of creation in the divine image is not relational in the sense of individual I-Thou relationality but communal. Thus the new humanity of God's coming future that is ours by grace is anticipated in the communion of saints, the church. He concludes, "The relational self is the ecclesial self."[27] This relativizes all relational structures as orders of history.

Miroslav Volf has much the same thing to say in his book *After Our Likeness: The Church as the Image of the Trinity*: "Because the Christian God is not a lonely God, but rather a communion of the three persons, faith leads human beings into divine *communion*. One cannot, however, have a self-enclosed communion with the triune God—a 'foursome,' as it were—for the Christian God is not a private deity."[28]

From the standpoint of creation as the arrival of God's future and the fulfillment of our creation in the image at that arrival, sexuality, as part of our drive toward bonding in love, is both fulfilled and transcended. In this paradigm, our humanity and our sexuality are *not yet* "ordered" but *on the way*—being transformed according to his image—until the ultimate communion and union with God and one another that is reflective of the *imago Trinitatis*. God, creating from the future, draws us by the grace of the Spirit toward that destiny.

In longing for the life of our future with God, our sexual lives, along with all human pursuits in the penultimate world of the *not yet*, are animated by love's quest for the values it seeks in anticipation of God's future revealed in Christ. Those values are life, the peace and wholeness of shalom, equality among all (justice), community (reconciliation), joy, and freedom from all bondage to sin and evil (personal, social, and political).[29] As we shall see, they are the values neighbor love pursues in sexual relations, as in all activities of life. Driven by love, it is a profoundly relational ethic applicable to all circumstances of sexual life as it seeks the fulfillment of its future in the final realization of God's design for creation. Furthermore, in our penultimate strivings, we have the ideal of spiritual-sexual unity Carr seeks expressed analogously in the unity of human and divine in the Christ in whom "we live and move and have our being" (Acts 17:28). As I shall now point out, it is a profoundly realistic ethic for life in the ambiguous realm of the not yet.

Orders of Anticipation and Christian Vocation

Because the values of God's promised future are at the heart of the gospel promise, Christian striving for them in Christlike love, both individually and corporately, is a genuine expression of God's good news. This witness to God's promises is the vocation of the universal priesthood.[30] Luther associated vocation in the ministry of the whole people of God. Our occupations in the orders of this world are the venues we have for the expression of that calling.

Following the focus on the promises of God's coming future, the term I would substitute for *orders of creation* is *orders of anticipation*. It signifies that our occupations and the historical institutions that order our lives are channels for seeking the goods of God's future in love for God, the neighbor, and the creation itself. As a people of anticipation, the Christian community reaches out to the future that is coming and, in so doing, gives witness to the hope that is within it.[31]

I would claim, then, that sexual ethics is the servant of the vocation of Christian witness and finds its meaning in the guidance it gives to our sexual lives as a people of anticipation. Having argued against the doctrine of marriage as an order of creation, I propose that marriage is best understood as an order of anticipation, an avenue of witness. If parenting is involved, that too is an order of anticipation.

The sexual bonding of persons marked by what Thielicke—I think rightly—called the interfusion of eros and agape anticipates values of life and wholeness, justice, freedom, and community. Though marriage is transcended eschatologically in community, it is one powerful penultimate anticipation of that community.

However, if the ethical witness of heterosexual marriage is grounded in a future that transcends it, it seems clear that other sorts of loving and just sexual relationships can also be orders of anticipation. This would include gay and lesbian unions, for example. The fact that same-sex marriage is now legal in this country, though most welcome, does not obviate the need for the theological argument on their behalf; that argument is still needed in the face of persistent religious opposition.

In our earlier discussion of cohabitation, a major concern raised against the practice by various Christian voices was the sort of witness it was giving. The issue is framed in terms of marriage as communal—a public witness to fidelity that helps build trust. By contrast, the argument is that cohabitation is individualistic, not communal, and therefore not an adequate expression of the public vocation of marriage. I quote from that chapter's reference to the sexuality social statement of the Evangelical Lutheran Church in America (ELCA): "Central to our vocation, in relation to human sexuality, is the building and protection of trust in relationships."[32] This vocation to build relationships of trust is not a private matter alone. It is part of the Christian witness in the community and the Christian's calling in all situations.[33]

While I am in total agreement with this defense of marriage, what we learn from taking on the "orders" of tradition and its natural law allies from the perspective of the future is that sexuality in the present is open to many forms of expression that can anticipate the values of the future that transcends and fulfills it. Again, marriage per se is neither an order of creation nor an eschatological expectation for the fulfillment of humanity. What is an anticipation of God's future is being formed in the love of Christ reaching out in longing for that day when God, who is love, "will be all in all" (1 Corinthians 15:28). That faithful seniors who are cohabiting can fulfill this vocation of anticipation seems clear to me in the openness of all things to God's future.

Likewise, the life of committed love and caring is possible for the elderly, married or unmarried, in long-term care communities. Their loving of one another is a witness to the gospel of God's boundless love and care for all. It reflects God's unconditional love revealed in the Christ and anticipates its final consummation. As older people make selfless adjustments to the limitations of age for the pleasure of one another, they bear witness to Jesus's self-giving love. Even when mental capacities are diminished, shared affection is a testimony to the promise of God's final shalom, when all are made whole. All these moments of tenderness, seen and unseen, anticipate the joy that is the promise of God's coming reign. They are a small, seemingly insignificant, but nonetheless true penultimate expression fueled by the grace of God that suffuses all of the creation on the way to its completion. Aging and loving lives toward the end in anticipation of the beginning.

However, the concept of anticipation signifies both having and not having. We seek to anticipate the ultimate promise in the penultimate forms of love but recognize that those efforts are always in a struggle with the reality of sin. Even as we celebrate the sexuality that older adults share with all humanity, they also share the temptations and impulses toward sexual activity that is selfish and exploitative. Thus orders of anticipation are ordered. There are and need to be norms that both judge and guide along with the Spirit that transforms and empowers what is truly loving. This is the task of the next chapter.

Further Thoughts

Grow old along with me!
The best is yet to be,
The last of life, for which the first was made:
Our times are in His hand
Who saith "A whole I planned,
Youth shows but half; trust God: see all, nor be afraid!"

These lines from the first stanza of Robert Browning's poem "Rabbi Ben Ezra" are probably some of the most quoted from all of Browning's work. In our discussion of aging, the temptation to quote them and look at the poem as a whole is too great to resist. What does it mean and how does it fit with our considerations about aging? In people's experience, is it really the case that "the best is yet to be"? Many would doubtless say the opposite as the ailments and diminished capacities of later life overtake the pleasures of younger days. The rabbi of Browning's poem invites us to look beyond the losses of old age and see it instead through the lens of faith in God. This is an optimistic declaration—a theological conviction—that God has a plan for the whole of life, and it is only at the end that we realize the completion of that plan. It is then that we experience that "best."

A reading of the entire poem reveals the poet's understanding of life as ambiguous, often conflictual, and paradoxical. But we are in God's hands. Throughout youth and into old age, God, as in the biblical image of the potter, is shaping the clay of our lives. With age we gain the wisdom that comes from dealing with the adversities of our youth. So the final stanza calls on God to fulfill the promise of the first stanza:

So, take and use Thy work:
Amend what flaws may lurk,
What strain o' the stuff, what warpings past the aim!
My times be in Thy hand!
Perfect the cup as planned!
Let age approve of youth, and death complete the same!

It is in the end, at death, that God's plan for us enters its fulfillment. There is comfort in that for Browning because of his belief that life continues beyond death. It is there that the "perfection of the cup" goes forward. The end is the beginning, the advent of the "new" for our lives.

At times in Browning's work, one senses that he thinks of life beyond death as a time for finishing what was left undone in life. The suggestion is there in this famous line from the poem "Andrea Del Sarto": "Ah, but a man's reach should exceed his grasp, or what's a heaven for?" In a lesser-known Browning poem, "Evelyn Hope," the poet speaks of his love for a young woman who died at an age too young for him to have pursued his love for her. Is this unexpressed love forever frustrated?

> *No, indeed! for God above*
> *Is great to grant, as mighty to make,*
> *And creates the love to reward the love:*
> *I claim you still, for my own love's sake!*
> Delayed it may be for more lives yet,
> Through worlds I shall traverse, not a few: *[emphasis mine]*
> *Much is to learn, much to forget*
> *Ere the time be come for taking you.*

Life after death, it seems, is a series of worlds within which what has not been realized on earth may yet find fulfillment beyond the pale of this life.

What was the true nature of Browning's faith? His theology? I can't be sure. I can only say what I have inferred from a few select lines of his poetry. While knowing the answer to those questions may be important to the scholarly study of Browning's life and work, words have a life of their own beyond their original meaning in the mind of the author. They have the power to enter our own time and consciousness and interact dialectally with our world of thought. What is striking for me is how well the rabbi's vision comports with the understanding I have laid out in this chapter—that God's future is drawing us toward the fulfillment of our creation in the image of God. The potter, the creator of Genesis 2, shaping humanity from the dust of the earth, completes that work in the arrival of the future, the completion of all creation.

The picture is not one of a once-perfected primordial humanity living disordered lives in a disordered world until they escape that world in life after death. Rather, the picture is one of the creator shaping that disordered life and world until the arrival of its future perfection, the "best that is yet to be." In the Christian faith, we may say that we are being transformed according to his image. Christ is with us along the way as we grow old, gaining in grace if not in wisdom. Ageism fails to see what Rabbi Ben Ezra saw—that age is not simply decline, whatever its outward manifestations; it is the successful end of a long and often perilous journey to fulfillment in the loving hands of the potter when the clay of our humanity rises with the Christ to the worlds of the new creation.

Chapter Six

Aging, Sexuality, and the Ethics of Christian Love

> There is no way toward the divine love except through the discovery of human intimacy and community. One feeds the other. Care of the soul, then, requires an openness to love's many forms.
>
> —Thomas Moore, *Care of the Soul*

> The life of the Christian community has as its rationale—if not invariably its practical reality—the task of teaching us to so order our relations that human beings may see themselves as desired, as the occasion of joy.
>
> —Rowan Williams

I have offered an argument for reframing the orders of creation tradition in terms of the eschatological perspective of the "orders of anticipation," which I propose is a responsible biblical theology in tune with our modern understanding of reality as historical, in process, and open to the future—for Christians, open to the coming of God's future reign. Within the openness of that framework in which we and all creation await and long for fulfillment, I have maintained that older adults of all sexual orientations can be faithful to their Christian vocation of witness to the love of Christ in a variety of committed, loving, and just relationships when traditional marriage may not be a meaningful alternative.

I also want to make clear, if I have not already done so, that I want to lift up the value of marriage and celebrate those of all sexual orientations who are blessed with a loving marriage to the end of life and those who are able to be happily remarried in later life. That said, my assertion that the same blend of agape and eros can find expression outside of that formal covenant needs to be tested by the ethics of agape love. What are the norms of love that guide our sexual relationships and how do they apply in later life situations? Moreover, how does our engagement with the ethics of love in later life speak also to the conduct and outlook of family, friends, caregivers, and those who minister to older adults? We have already said a good bit about Christian love and sexuality, but a more formal treatment in the light of those questions is needed.

Before we take these next steps in our journey, it is necessary, I think, to clarify what we mean when we speak of sexual or intimate relationships in later life. Recall Merryn Gott's concern (see chapter 2) that judging older-adult sexual expression by the "gold standard" of intercourse fails to appreciate the different ways in which older people share sexual intimacy. We are well aware that sexual expression in older age runs the gamut of cuddling, loving touch, hugging and kissing, manual mutual pleasuring, oral sex, and so on. It may or may not involve intercourse. And if it does not, it is no less a genuine sexual relationship. To think otherwise is to trivialize the precious and loving reality of that coupling—ageism once again.

To illustrate the point, I recall an incident that occurred while I was engaged in our church's sexuality study. A retired pastor came to me who was widowed and in love with another older woman whose husband had died. He asked if the church had some kind of public ceremony that could bless their union even though legal marriage was impractical. Having such a ceremony was important to them as Christian people with a deep moral sense. "After all, we just want to be together," he said. "We just cuddle; intercourse is not possible." His rationale was that if they weren't having sexual intercourse, there seemed no reason why their relationship shouldn't be blessed by the church; in the absence of intercourse, it didn't entail the church's normal policy of blessing only legal marriages.

At the time, I had nothing to offer by way of ceremony. I wished I had. Looking back on this encounter, I now would say his thinking was a bit contradictory. He and his partner were correct in thinking of their relationship as a truly committed union worthy of public blessing, even in the absence of intercourse. However, at the same time, he seemed to be suggesting that some sort of ceremony, in a separate category from marriage, should be possible because they weren't having intercourse. The point is that all truly committed loving and just relationships in which marriage is not an option—regardless of the manner of sexual expression or the couple's sexual orientation—are under the same obligations of Christian love we would expect of traditional marriage.

Agape: Values, Virtues, and Norms

The values, virtues, and norms of the agape love Christ embodied, commanded, and empowered are a beacon showing the way to God's future and a compass to navigate the journey with the wind of the Spirit at our backs.

Agape: Love

Agape is the love God has for the world (John 3:16). Agape is the love Jesus has shown for us and we, in turn, are to show one another (John 13:34). Agape is the foundational norm of the Christian faith and life: "'You shall love the Lord your God with all your heart, and with all your soul, and with all your mind.' This is the greatest and first commandment. And a second is like it: 'You shall love your neighbor as yourself.' On these two commandments hang all the law and the prophets" (Matthew 22:37–40; see also Mark 12:30–31; Luke 10:27).

A great deal has been written about agape, what it means and what it entails. I will speak of it as I have in previous writings in terms of its *outlook*, *disposition*, and *objective*.[1] In discussing each of these aspects of agape, I want to relate them (1) to the principles or general rules of love (*respect for autonomy*, *justice*, *sanctity of life*, *promise-keeping*, *truth-telling*) that give further definition to how love acts; (2) to the virtues, inspired by the Beatitudes, which express the sorts of persons we are with a character formed by love (*poverty of spirit, solidarity in suffering, mercy, peace-making*); and (3) to the values of God's coming reign introduced in the previous chapter as revealed in the person and work of Jesus the Christ, values that love anticipates (*life, the peace and wholeness of shalom, equality among all* [*justice*], *community* [*reconciliation*], *joy*, and *freedom from all bondage to sin and evil* [*personal, social,* and *political*]).

AGAPE: OUTLOOK

In terms of outlook, agape is *universal* in scope, or *all inclusive*. The key passage here is Matthew 5:43–44: "You have heard that it was said, 'You shall love your neighbor and hate your enemy.' But I say to you, Love your enemies and pray for those who persecute you." If one's enemies are not excluded, who could be? Agape love, love of neighbor, considers all as our neighbors. The parallel in Luke 6:27–28 serves to underscore this outlook: "But I say to you that listen, Love your enemies, do good to those who hate you, bless those who curse you, pray for those who abuse you." All are to be held in equal regard without prejudice. The love of God in Christ is unconditional, extending to us in our sinfulness. Paul says in Romans 5:8, "But God proves his love for us in that while we still were sinners Christ died for us." As God's love is unconditional, so should ours be as well.

Sanctity of Life

God's unconditional love is a sign of the sanctity of all life. Nowhere is this more clearly revealed than in the event of the Christ's death and resurrection. The resurrection victory reveals the triumph of everlasting life as the paramount value of the coming reign of God, which love anticipates in its unconditional regard for the sanctity of all life.

Love's commitment to the sanctity of life also looks toward the fullness of God's shalom, the peace marked by relational wholeness and wholeness of body and spirit in the resurrection of the whole person, anticipated in Jesus's works of healing and restoration to fellowship of those he healed (Mark 1:35–45; Matthew 9:1–8; Luke 5:17–26).

Life is holy from start to finish. Love entails respect for that fact in terms of care for the aged—not only their physical and spiritual well-being but also their needs for intimacy, which is so integral to life itself. The bonding of love with another in acts of sexual intimacy is an essential part of life's wholeness and vitality. To dismiss sexual expression in later life as nonessential or even disgusting fails the test of love's commitment to the triumph of life in its fullness. For some, I suppose the sight of a staff member in a nursing home helping someone into a bed in order for him to have some intimate moments of sexual sharing and lovemaking with a woman he has come to know and love may be disturbing. But from love's vantage point, it is a moment for affirming the sanctity of life in the fullness of its lifelong sexuality.

We have heard the voices of those Christian traditions that condemn any sexual activity outside marriage regardless of age. Rules against extramarital sex and the insistence upon legal marriage as the only fit context for shared sexual expression have their place in the ethics of love. The Christian ethic lives with the realization that we are an already-not-yet people. We are redeemed by the grace of God in Christ, but we are not yet fully formed in the image of our destiny with God; we are still struggling with sin. These rules exist to curb our inclinations toward promiscuity and unfaithfulness and serve to protect the well-being of our children. More positively, among other things, marriage, legally confirmed and publicly blessed, serves as a witness to the sanctity of our sexual lives. It is one order of anticipation among other stations of life.

Does the rationale of insisting on legal marriage have the same force among older adults for whom marriage is not a meaningful option and having children is in the past? I have already made the case that legal marriage is not necessary in all cases for Christians to fulfill their vocation. To that argument, I would now add the further contention that condemning sexual intimacy in a loving and just relationship in later life because there is no legal marriage may do more harm than good by arbitrarily preventing the sharing of life-affirming intimacy or casting a pall over its values as a witness to a truly loving and just union.

Loving and *just* are the key terms here. Marriage is supposed to ensure those values through promises made. That purpose of marriage carries over into all unions of later life. From start to finish, our sexual lives, if they show love's respect for the sanctity of life, will seek always to be loving and just. To aspire to that commitment in our sexual lives is to seek always the integrity of life as an intimate blend of spiritual and physical.

Justice

Love's embrace of justice in our sexual relationships is critical to a faithful expression of our spiritual-physical unity, the interfusion of eros and agape (Thielicke) and its corollary in sexual-spiritual unity (Carr). Otherwise, relationships become a matter of mutual exploitation rather than truly caring and just, something that can happen inside marriage as well as outside.

The all-inclusive and unconditional nature of agape love requires an egalitarian justice in which all are of equal value. This is a *principle* of love's conduct and a promised *value* of God's future reign in which "there is no longer Jew or Greek, there is no longer slave or free, there is no longer male and female; for all of you are one in Christ Jesus" (Galatians 3:28). This means that justice demands equal regard in our relationships in general and our sexual relationships in particular.

Central to the justice of equality is another principle of love: *respect for autonomy.* Respect for autonomy is respect for the fact that we are created in the image of God, as we have said earlier, with the endowments of personhood: freedom and responsibility. Sexual relations that are truly consensual are those in which the partners respect the autonomy of each other. Recall the discussion in chapter 4 about the tests to determine whether those with dementia or cognitive impairment have the capacity to consent. The various assessments proposed are grounded in respect for autonomy. In long-term care facilities, testing capacity is also a legal concern, as consent is required to protect the residents' rights and prevent harm. However, in all sexual relations, consenting to one another's sexual desires is a mark of love's justice. In older age, when past patterns of sexual expression are no longer possible either in kind or in frequency, it is perhaps more important than ever to be deliberate in seeking to find each other sexually, particularly if the partners are not of equal health and vigor.

In her excellent discussion of sexual justice, when Margaret Farley addresses the injunctions to do no harm, to respect autonomy, and to ensure free consent, she talks of treating people as "ends in themselves."[2] This echo of Kant's categorical imperative comports well with the love commandment's commitment to all, even one's enemies. It enjoins us to treat others not merely as means to our own ends but always as persons who have ends of their own. So it should be in the sharing of our sexual lives and the desires we express to one another. The self-centeredness of human nature is always capable of using the other to satisfy one's own sexual needs without due regard for the will of the other.

Does the medical enhancement of male sexual performance run the risk of men focusing more on their own performance more than the needs of their partner? Does the fact that women outnumber men among older adults create a real danger of the sort of patriarchal context in which men take advantage of the situation at the expense of women? These fears were raised in chapter 2. To the extent that they are real fears, they pose a clear issue for love's commitment to sexual justice and gender equality. The danger is real, since for the oldest age cohort, gender inequality was a fact of life and not as challenged as it has been in recent times. My mother repeatedly told me "It's a man's world"—seemingly without much regret. At the same time, at least some older folks drawn together by the leveling experiences of old age may become examples of genuine egalitarian mutuality in their feelings for one another, anticipating in their own way the promise that "there is no longer male and female; for all of you are one in Christ Jesus" (Galatians 3:28).

In truth, it is difficult for any of us to completely avoid the problem of self-centeredness in our sex lives. We do engage in sexual activity in the hope of our pleasure being satisfied, which is normal and healthy. However, at times, our own drives can crowd out our consideration for the needs of our partner. That said, the ideal is ever before us, calling us forward by grace as we grow in love as kind and considerate lovers. As we noted earlier, older lovers often say that they are more patient, tolerant, and understanding than in their youth, with the result that sex seems better than ever. Rather than devalue, deny, or make fun of the sexuality of older adults, perhaps we have something to learn from them!

In addition to sexual justice in our personal relationships, it is important to pay attention to sexual justice in our social relationships. Love anticipates the promise of total equality in God's future when it refuses to countenance and indeed fights against all the "isms" in this world that oppress people with their prejudicial attitudes and actions. In our conversation, we have repeatedly noted the harmful effects of ageism and heterosexism. Where such prejudicial attitudes exist in the Christian church, the justice of agape love requires that it be called out. Those directly involved with the aged and the LGBTQ community need to be educated and better attuned to the lives of these people. Thankfully, we have seen evidence of this happening in some faith-based long-term care communities with clear policies and practices. But we also heard from researchers that more education is required for greater understanding and acceptance to prevail. Advocacy by such organizations as SAGE, which we spoke of in chapter 4, along with the Human Rights Campaign Foundation and others, serves this value of justice.

The Virtues of Love: Poverty of Spirit

The Sermon on the Mount is Jesus's messianic manifesto. He is claiming authority to preach a more radical understanding of God's law, but also, because *he* is here, bringing in the promises of God's coming reign, the commands are now possibilities, not simply demands or judgments. One biblical scholar has captured this momentous truth by proposing that in the Beatitudes, *blessed* might well be translated *congratulations*.[3] These qualities of the spirit, grounded in the person and work of Jesus himself, are conferred by grace and lived out by grace. "Congratulations, you can be poor in spirit!" "Congratulations, you can be merciful!" "Congratulations, you can be a peacemaker!" That's the sense of it. We are formed in the virtues of love for the life of love.

"Blessed are the poor in spirit, for theirs is the kingdom of heaven" (Matthew 5:3). This is the first of the Beatitudes and, in many respects, sets the tone for all the Beatitudes and for all that we have said thus far about the life of love. The noted Latin American theologian Gustavo Gutiérrez has defined poverty of spirit as related to the gospel theme of spiritual childhood, a trusting faith that receives the gift of God's grace with open arms.[4] The gift of poverty of spirit is the gift of a spirit without pretense or arrogance that gladly recognizes that its life is wholly dependent on the grace of God. Arrogance and pretense are self-protective. In the confidence of God's favor, poverty of spirit reaches out to take the risks of love in a combination of humility and courage. All we have just discussed about the all-inclusive and unconditional outlook of agape love and its commitment to the sanctity of life and justice in both personal and social relations would not be possible without the openness to the other that is poverty of spirit.

Agape: Self-Giving

The humility and openness to the other in poverty of spirit leads us directly to the *disposition* of agape: it is *self-giving.* Once again, Jesus is the model, as Paul sets forth in the beautiful Christ hymn of Philippians 2:5–11:

> *Let the same mind be in you that was in Christ Jesus,*
>
> *who, though he was in the form of God,*
> *did not regard equality with God*
> *as something to be exploited,*
> *but emptied himself,*
> *taking the form of a slave,*
> *being born in human likeness.*
> *And being found in human form,*
> *he humbled himself*
> *and became obedient to the point of death—*
> *even death on a cross.*
>
> *Therefore God also highly exalted him*
> *and gave him the name*
> *that is above every name,*
> *so that at the name of Jesus*
> *every knee should bend,*
> *in heaven and on earth and under the earth,*
> *and every tongue should confess*
> *that Jesus Christ is Lord,*
> *to the glory of God the Father.*

As the Christ is exalted for his self-giving sacrifice, so God extols the life of self-giving neighbor love. However, before we move into a discussion of what that means for our concerns in this narrative, we need to remember that the commandment says "love your neighbor *as yourself*" (Matthew 22:39; emphasis mine).

Loving yourself takes on special importance in old age, as Frits de Lange has helped us see. What does it mean to love oneself? The answer is in what he deems to be the first commandment: "Love life as it is given to you."[5] Your life is a gift of God to be loved as we are to love God, for to love the gift of life is to love the God who gives it. Love of self in this sense is a testimony to the worth of your life as God given. Love of self in this understanding is also a stepping-stone to love of neighbor; the three elements of the command to love—God, self, and neighbor—are intertwined. De Lange likes this reading: "Love your neighbor as another self. And yourself as another neighbor."[6]

These admonitions have special relevance to aging and the aged. De Lange makes a point that corresponds to the assumptions we have been operating with since the start of this book. The decline of physical or mental capacities that comes with age does not diminish human worth: "Therefore, until our last breath, we share in the divine dignity of human life."[7] At the same time, in old age, many of us have to cope with the realities of serious health problems. In light of this inescapable truth, de Lange thinks "health" should be defined more subjectively than by clinical standards. In old age, health might better be described in terms of the ability to cope with the ailments of age with a will to continue affirming life. Perhaps this is what Karl Barth meant by having "the strength for human life."[8]

Loving the self we are given involves staying friends with yourself in the face of the danger of lost self-esteem. The old can fall out of love with themselves. Thus the most fundamental care for the elderly is to help them continue to care about themselves—their bodies, their relationships, their daily lives, their pasts and futures, and their roles in society.[9]

De Lange's understanding of the meaning of love for self when it comes to the aged fits nicely with our assertion of lifelong dignity and destiny in God's image. It also correlates with our observations of the harmful effects of ageism. When the aged internalize the denigrating images and stereotypes about them, they can, as de Lange puts it, fall out of love with themselves. Assault on the integrity of sexual life in old age can be a particularly cutting attack on self-esteem. Insofar as it is a painful blow to one's self-worth, it can hamper the ability to love others. I am bold to quote myself at this point: "Self-giving love requires a self to give. Sacrificial love for the neighbor is meaningless unless we possess and care for the self that we offer. In creation and redemption God has given us life, our selves. We are called upon to cherish and care for this precious gift, not to neglect our well-being or consider ourselves of no account. Out of the freedom and confidence of knowing our worth as children of God we are able to give love."[10]

The courage to love oneself in old age so as to also love one's neighbor is a grace that points to another of love's self-giving virtues: *solidarity in suffering*. "Blessed are those who mourn, for they shall be comforted" (Matthew 5:4) is the beatitude that gives rise to this expression of love. The capacity to mourn comes from being in the sort of relationship with others that is marked by a deep, empathic sense of connection. This is the intimate relatedness of agape, reflective of God's self-giving relation to all of creation, analogous to the mutual self-giving love of the persons of the Trinity. Without this sense of connection, there is no sense of loss or sorrow. However, mourning is not only what we feel at the loss of a loved one or even the lost lives of war or natural disaster. It is also a sensitivity to suffering of all sorts, a solidarity with the suffering of others that is reflective of Jesus's solidarity with our suffering. Jesus not only wept at the grave of Lazarus, whom he loved; he wept for us (Luke 19:4–42), loved us all, and took the burden of human brokenness to the cross and into the divine life in solidarity with our suffering and death. Once again, the beatitudes have their deepest meaning when referred to the Christ.

The aged tend to experience more loss and suffering than they did in younger years. Death and illness become regular parts of one's life. Older couples in intimate relationships practice the virtue of solidarity in suffering by reaching out to each other with sensitivity to each other's needs, with each member making the other's trials, pains, and limitations their own in their lives together. This includes their sexual lives in whatever forms of intimacy they may take, for this intimacy is at the core of life. We saw couples make loving adjustments to one another's sexual capacities in the face of illness or other physical limitations, as illustrated in some of the interviews in Connie Goldman's collection (chapter 2). Mutual accommodations in the sharing of sexual intimacy are prevalent in long-term care communities. These acts of sensitivity represent a pattern of self-giving love.

Self-giving love is the capacity to care about the other for their own sake—to treat them as ends in themselves (Farley). This is about compassion, "suffering with." In the Gospels, Jesus feels compassion for the crowd gathered and heals their sick (Matthew 14:14) and shows compassion for the widow of Nain as she weeps after the death of her only son (Luke 7:13). And for us, we have this encouragement: "As God's chosen ones, holy and beloved, clothe yourselves with compassion, kindness, humility, meekness, and patience" (Colossians 3:12).

Where the sort of solidarity in self-giving love we have been speaking of is present in the lives of older couples—whether married, cohabiting, or in long-term care communities—one can hardly gainsay its essential holiness. Self-giving, we know, is often crowded by natural inclinations to self-centeredness, and older folks are not immune. But as they confront the pains and challenges of change in later life, there is grace for the way; the Beatitudes promise comfort—which is to say the strength and grace of Emmanuel, God with us in solidarity with our every joy and sorrow. Family members, friends, and caregivers can be conduits of that grace.

A stark contrast to the ideal we are projecting is the self-serving example in Robert Youdin's story of Marvin (chapter 4). Marvin's promiscuity, encouraged by Linda, his first sexual partner, led to an STD. STDs are a common problem for the freewheeling sexual lives of many older adults. Marvin is not exceptional in that regard. Marvin's reaction was not of remorse but of embarrassment at having to admit he carried a disease to his partners. His change was not a change of heart but a change of practice—use of condoms—in order to resume his previous sexual adventures. I am seeking a Christian sexual ethic for those in later life that is liberating, responsible, and sensitive to their life situations. I am not talking about liberation from all norms of love and justice in sexual life. The film *Cloud 9*, while lifting up the vitality of sexuality in older age, also records the tragedy of broken promises with desire run amok.

The ethics of self-giving love in the spirit of solidarity anticipates two values of God's future: *freedom* and *joy*. Total freedom from all forms of bondage, even the bondage of sin, awaits the finality of God's reign. Total joy in the absence of sorrow also awaits that future when all tears will be wiped away (Revelation 21:4). The promise of God's future is with us now in the freedom and joy of divine forgiveness, but the fullness of that promise still belongs to the future. Still, even in this not yet time, by God's grace we can experience a foretaste of that ultimate beatitude. I speak of freedom from bondage to self-centered and selfish desires and the joy of God's blessing reflected in the joy of one's beloved—the joy of knowing that you have truly and freely given of yourself to their physical pleasure and emotional well-being. However penultimate in their perfection, God is with us in our efforts to truly love. Amid all the failures and perversion of this life, I believe love prevails. Loving in later life seems to be a testimony to that conviction: "Set me as a seal upon your heart, as a seal upon your arm; for love is strong as death, passion fierce as the grave. Its flashes are flashes of fire, a raging flame. Many waters cannot quench love, neither can floods drown it. If one offered for love all the wealth of his house, it would be utterly scorned" (Song of Solomon 8:6–7).

Agape: Communion and Union

The objective or goal of agape is *communion and union* with God and with each other. Paul Tillich has characterized agape "as the drive toward the reunion of the separated."[11] Agape's drive toward communion and union is an anticipation of the *value* of communion and union with God and one another, which is a promise of the coming reign of God. Thus we have these words from Paul to the Corinthian congregation and to us: "All this is from God, who reconciled us to himself through Christ, and has given us the ministry of reconciliation; that is, in Christ God was reconciling the world to himself, not counting their trespasses against them, and entrusting the message of reconciliation to us" (2 Corinthians 5:18–19).

God's reconciling love has brought us together with God, back from the alienation of sin. We, in turn, seek in love to establish communion and union with and among our neighbors. This is the "message of reconciliation" in action.

God's reconciling love in Christ is the outpouring of divine mercy. It follows that our reconciling love should be an expression of the *virtue of mercy* bestowed in this beatitude: "Blessed are the merciful, for they will receive mercy" (Matthew 5:7). Its companion virtue in the drive toward communion and union anticipates the peace that is a promise of God's coming reign: "Blessed are the peacemakers, for they will be called children of God" (Matthew 5:9). Mercy and the *virtue of peacemaking* go together in love's quest for the reunion of the separated.

In our engagement with the relational concerns of intimacy in later life, a paramount expression of mercy—so vital to peacemaking among individuals—is *forgiveness*. Once again, the beatitude on mercy and its connection to forgiveness refer us back to the Christ who bestows his blessing of new possibility for those who would follow him. Undeserving though we are in so many ways, a merciful and forgiving God, out of compassion for us, supplies our needs and continually renews the divine promise of life everlasting. God's mercy is an expression of the divine, unconditional love that is so graphically presented in the parable of the prodigal son (Luke 15:11–24). Add to that, and many other biblical statements of God's forgiveness, this concise statement in the Letter to the Ephesians: "In him we have redemption through his blood, the forgiveness of our trespasses, according to the riches of his grace" (Ephesians 1:7).

In the crucifixion, the truly human Jesus's solidarity with the sin and death of our humanity was total. In that unspeakably brutal event, Jesus's unity with the Father and the Spirit was also total. The pain of our estrangement from God overflowed in his cry, "My God, my God, why have you forsaken me" (Matthew 27:46; Mark 15:34). Our estrangement had become his estrangement, an experience in the life of the Triune God. Jesus's death was an event in the divine life of the Trinity. If God does not take our suffering and death into God's own experience, one could hardly call God loving, for love is deeply affected by the pain of the beloved. What parent seeing their child being hurt or suffering an illness does not fervently wish it were her own pain? So it is with God, our loving parent, who *did* take our pain to its end so that it is no longer ours and can be wiped away in the healing touch of forgiveness.

As with God's forgiveness, so also with ours; forgiveness creates a new state of affairs. With the prodigal son, the father's forgiveness brought him from death to life, from estrangement to renewed sonship. Our readiness to forgive has that same capacity to change the state of affairs and fulfill agape's goal of reuniting the separated. In life's most intimate relationships, it is inevitable that at times we will disappoint or hurt the other person, or vice versa. If that relationship is to last, there must be both a desire for forgiveness and a willingness to forgive. To be truly a source of renewed bonding, forgiveness must be more than simply letting the other person off the hook. It must be an expression of the unconditional love we see in the prodigal son's father. This is a stretch for our human capacities. Hurts have a way of staying with us and leaving their mark. If forgiveness is half-hearted, it is likely that hurts may simply be shelved temporarily, only to be brought out again as ammunition when the next conflict arises. Even though we may forgive and try to purge our hearts of anger and a sense of alienation from the other, the task is not easy.

In old age, when we look over the landscape of many years, we may see it cluttered with failures of love and justice, broken relationships, betrayals and lies. These are the memories that haunt one during sleepless nights. In the end, only God's promise of mercy can ease the pain of those terrifying thoughts. In this, there is hope and peace. However, if throughout the many conflicts endured and hurts inflicted forgiveness is ungiven and unbidden, God's grace will seem far away and bitterness close at hand. By contrast, in the light of God's mercy, the experiences of one's long life, looked at honestly and repentantly, can be a source of readiness to forgive and accept persons as they are, just as God does.

The grace older lovers must have to accept each other as they are is a form of unspoken forgiveness, a way of life that makes for peace. It is a profound habit of the commitment of love, whether inside or outside of formal marriage. In *Cloud 9*, Inge could not accept Werner for who he was—a quiet and, one infers, a dull man, but faithful over the decades. The movie even shows him making love to Inge at her prompting. He wasn't incapable of responding to his wife. However, he is still no match for the charms of a vigorous and lively Karl.

Both *truth-telling* and *promise-keeping*, principles of love, are essential to love's drive toward communion and union. Both are critical to creating the trust that is the glue holding truly mutual unions together. Falsehood and betrayal are hardly the pathways to reconciliation or a sustained and loving relationship. Arguably, truth-telling and promise-keeping, vital to all relationships, are the only bases of trust in later-life relationships outside the bonds of legal marriage. (A public legal commitment to marriage is no guarantee of truthfulness and faithfulness, although it can be a hedge against dissolution even in these days of easier divorce.)

Truth-telling begins with an honest evaluation of one's motives and behavior. Examining one's motives for cohabitation seems particularly important. I make no attempt to adjudicate which reasons are morally acceptable and which are not. I have argued for the possibility that sexual unions in later life that are just and loving can be ethically responsible when marriage is not a meaningful option. Here are some questions couples can ask of themselves to test that claim:

- Has the couple made a truthful assessment of their motives for the decision to cohabit?
- Have they been honest with one another about the failures of past relationships if there were such?
- Can they honestly say that there are no unresolved issues of past marriages that could compromise their ability to make a healthy new start?
- Do they trust each other's intentions to be truly loving in sharing their lives and sexual lives together?
- Can they truthfully make promises to each other of a genuine love that embraces justice in granting mutual equality, that respects autonomy, and that is self-giving in commitment to and sensitivity to the needs of the other?
- Are these commitments at work in their sexual lives, blending eros and agape?
- Are they ready to care for each other in tough times to the best of their ability?

These are the same promises entailed in the vows of marriage. Making and abiding by these promises is a clear expression of agape's unconditional commitment.

Can such promises really be sustained without legal bonds? The studies we looked at in chapter 3 indicated that cohabiting relationships among older adults were quite stable and satisfying. As the studies report, older adults who cohabit rarely break up. The end of the relationship is most likely to be the death of a partner.

We have looked at the reactions to cohabitation on the part of various church bodies. In most cases, they are not thoroughly convinced by the prospects of a loving, just, and sustained cohabiting relationship in later life. However, the Episcopal Church USA (ECUSA) has taken that possibility seriously. In chapter 3, we reviewed the resolution of the 79th General Convention in 2018 proposing the development of a liturgy, "The Blessing of a Lifelong Relationship," to formalize committed relationships outside of marriage. We also sampled the rationale of "households," offered by some as possible support for a rite blessing lifelong relationships outside of marriage. The resolution, as reported earlier, is in committee at this writing. However, a companion resolution on pastoral resources reveals more about the church's thinking. The first two resolves are directly related to our present discussion:

> **A087 Develop Relationship Pastoral Resources**
>
> *Resolved,* That the 79th General Convention seeks to minister to the growing number of persons entering into sexually intimate relationships other than marriage, while acknowledging the Church's teaching on marriage, by calling for the curation and increased awareness of resources that provide pastoral guidance and teaching on relationships that involve sexual expression; and be it further
>
> *Resolved,* That the selection process for resources shall be guided by the following principles that were adopted by General Convention 2000-D039: "That we expect such relationships will be characterized by fidelity, monogamy, mutual affection and respect, careful, honest communication, and the holy love which enables those in such relationships to see in each other the image of God."

We don't know at this writing what will come of this initiative. On the one hand, the church has an obligation to uphold the value of marriage and ministry to the married; on the other hand, it has an obligation to minister to those in relationships outside marriage. These twin obligations of ministry represent an apparent conflict. The ECUSA proposal for a new rite with appropriate pastoral resources is, I think, a serious effort to resolve that conflict in a manner that preserves the values shared in both marriage and lifelong relationships outside marriage. It strikes one as a salutary prospect for relationships in later life, for cohabiting couples, and for couples in long-term care communities. However, the danger is that it could undermine the priority of marriage for younger people for whom marriage is a real possibility.

Regardless of whether these resolutions are finally approved as part of church practice, they have raised the issue of changing relational dynamics in today's world in a pronounced way. That said, neither this initiative nor any other church teaching that I have been able to discover makes the ethical distinction between those of an age who clearly have a path to marriage and those older adults in the third and fourth stages of life for whom marriage is not a meaningful option.

While cohabitation is still more prevalent among the younger generations, once again, research tells us that 63 percent of "baby boomers" (those born between 1944 and 1964) think cohabitation is a good idea. Even though religious persons in general are less likely to agree, the churches still face a growing population of older adults who may think cohabitation is a good option.[12] Establishing new rites may be fraught with ecclesial complications, but pastors could be set free to use their discretion to provide a public or private blessing to cohabiting older adults. Pastoral discretion was often exercised to bless same-sex unions prior to the legalization of same-sex marriage and is so today in matters of cohabitation when couples desire it. This should be welcomed. What is essential in the final analysis is the sort of just and loving commitment we have been discussing.

Final Thoughts

Aging and Loving

As I write these final thoughts, we are in the midst of the COVID-19 pandemic. People are sheltered at home and when outside must keep what is called "social distance." We are not supposed to touch anyone outside our own household—no handshakes or hugs, no passing the peace in church. We miss this human contact. Those who live alone, as so many of the elderly do, are bereft of touch, of contact with the warmth of another. They are continually being reminded that because of their age, they are at high risk for serious or fatal illness should they be exposed to the virus. Long-term care communities have been hit particularly hard by the virus so that many of its victims have been isolated in order to protect others from infection. People who die from the virus are dying alone, save for the kindness of medical staff, dying without the touch of their loved ones. To experience the privation of physical contact is to experience the loss of something life sustaining, life affirming, and even life giving.

Jesus's touch was both healing and life giving. He cleansed the leper with his touch (Matthew 8:3; Mark 1:41; Luke 5:13). At his touch, the fever left Peter's mother-in-law. He touched the eyes of the blind, and they could see (Matthew 20:34; Mark 8:22–25). Even those who were thought dead came alive at Jesus's touch (Luke 7:14; Matthew 9:25). There was a blessing in Jesus's touch so that people brought their children (Mark 10:13) and even infants (Luke 18:15) to him.

Jesus's compassionate and loving touch brought healing, life, and blessing. Touch was important to him, and it is to us. Our touch does not have the power of Jesus's touch, but it is in its own way life affirming and healing when it is done in love—a penultimate intimation of the ultimate. A tender embrace is able to communicate love in ways that words alone cannot. Jesus was not just God with us in preaching. Jesus was with us, God deep in our flesh, who continues to be with us in his real presence in the Eucharist.

Woven into the fabric of aging and loving is the intimacy of touch. The basic premise of all that has been said is that loving continues throughout aging. Thus it has been necessary to celebrate the sexuality of older adults and its physical expression, lest those who do not see or understand get in the way. Of course, it has been about not the physical contact of intimacy in and of itself but the blend of that touching with the virtues of self-giving love. This is also the love that values its own aged life as it is, continually adjusting its vocation to the changes of aging as it is drawn ever closer to the future.

I remember a woman I shall call Anna. She was very old, and I was very young—a young seminarian in his clinical term assigned to certain patients at the state mental hospital. Anna had a long history of being in and out of the facility. Her file was thick, and many of the documents were yellowed with age. Each time she was returned to her family, some incident would occur that sent her into an emotional tailspin from which she could not recover.

When I first met Anna, she was back in the hospital after one such event. She had by then outlived her family but not her enduring mental illness. She was in the hospital for the duration, and the duration was becoming increasingly unendurable. She was blind, alone, and now also suffering from a variety of ailments that often come with advanced age. Therefore, she was consigned to that ward in the hospital for those who had a combination of mental and physical problems. It was the closest thing to bedlam I had ever experienced; a constant cacophony of cries and groans.

During those times together, she spoke always of her suffering, of lying in bed in the darkness of her own visual and emotional night, constantly hearing the screams and groans of those around her. In the grip of fear, misery, and loneliness, she cried easily and often. She wanted to die. Yet in her darkness, the light of faith still burned, and this light, it seems, she could see clearly. There was no doubt in her mind that Jesus knew her sufferings, that God loved her and had a home for her. So we sat together each week, the cries of others all around us, and I listened to her refrain of relentless inner pain. I held her hand, and we prayed for death to come quickly, and with a word of God's forgiveness and a sign of the cross, we thanked God for the promise of new life.

As a young seminarian, I felt pretty ineffectual, and only in retrospect have I come to fully appreciate what happened between us. I am certain that holding hands as we prayed made all the difference. It did not restore her sight as Jesus's touch might have or quiet the storms in her head. However, it did create a real feeling of connection for the sharing of deeply intimate feelings of both sorrow and hope. And through her hand, it seemed that the energy of her faith flooded my inexperienced and anxious young mind. Anna—very old, blind, and literally at her wit's end—touched me and taught me. One's vocation, one's calling to exude the grace of God, knows no end.

The intimate touch of loving sexual expression should be understood as a part of all forms of human touch that are loving and life-affirming. There is nothing about holding the hand of a dying, suffering person that is sexual. But the touch of comfort and caring and the touch of sexual expression are deeply related as part of the communion and union of one with another that is love, a foretaste of our destiny. So unless we want to quit on life, we will never quit on loving.

APPENDIX

Pornography and Sexual Self-Pleasuring

The use of pornography and sexual self-pleasuring or masturbation are common practices among all age groups, including older adults. Because these practices are part of the sexual interest and sexual expression of adults in later life, they should not go unmentioned in our discussion. However, since the bulk of the narrative of this book involves relationships, I have chosen to place this discussion in an appendix.

The two largest Protestant denominations, the Southern Baptist Convention and the United Methodist Church (UMC), have no official position on masturbation.[1] The practice is not mentioned in the Evangelical Lutheran Church in America (ELCA) social statement *Human Sexuality: Gift and Trust*. The Anglican Church takes no position on the subject. The Presbyterian Church USA in 1991 called for the repudiation of damaging teaching about masturbation and a more positive view of its role in human sexuality. A number of evangelical churches have taken no official position because the Bible does not speak directly about it.[2] While there are mixed views among Protestant churches, there has certainly been a lessening of concern about sexual self-pleasuring. One might say that since the Kinsey studies (1948 and 1953), the practice has been demythologized, set free from false claims about its consequences and its status as a taboo.

The Roman Catholic Church, however, has maintained an official teaching that strongly condemns masturbation: "Within the Church's teaching on human sexuality, masturbation is considered to be objectively disordered or intrinsically evil (*in se malum* or *intrinsece malum*); that is, no circumstances or intentions can render the action of masturbation 'morally good.'"[3]

For the Catholic tradition, masturbation is an "unnatural" use of our sexual organs. But this view has not gone unchallenged in Catholic circles. Margaret Farley is one of the most prominent figures in this turn from traditional teaching. She notes that though some theologians still regard masturbation as immoral, many, if not most, along with medical professionals, regard it as morally neutral. Moreover, she observes that many women in more recent times have found great benefit from self-pleasuring, "especially in the discovery of their own possibilities for pleasure—something many had not experienced or even known about in their ordinary sexual relations with husbands or lovers."[4]

While many church bodies, ethicists, and certainly the general public have come to accept masturbation as morally neutral, the pornography with which the practice is often associated has not escaped censure. Here is an excerpt from the *Book of Discipline* of the UMC: "We oppose all forms of pornography and consider its use a form of sexual misconduct. Pornography is sexually explicit material that portrays violence, abuse, coercion, domination, humiliation, or degradation for the purpose of sexual arousal. Pornography sexually exploits and objectifies both women and men."[5]

The ELCA's *Message on . . . Commercial Sexual Exploitation* condemns all commercial uses of sex, such as prostitution, strip clubs, escort services, and for our immediate discussion, pornography. The use of pornographic material is not an individual sin alone; it is a social sin as well because it supports a multi-billion-dollar industry, a sex system that objectifies human beings as sex objects. As the document points out, "The sex system corrupts God's wonderful gift of sexuality by reducing it to a marketable item. It rips sex out of the mutual relationships of trust, love, and equality intended by God and mocks the faithful, caring, life-long marital context for sexual intimacy."[6]

These two statements from the UMC and the ELCA are typical of the stance taken by virtually all Christian church bodies. While there are certainly differences among individuals within these communions, the public antiporn position remains the overwhelming majority opinion of Christian communities.

Notwithstanding the objections of certain prominent faith traditions, the fact is that pornography is a flourishing industry that has mushroomed with the availability of online content—much of it free. We have also seen that the right to have erotic or pornographic materials is honored in long-term care facilities, regardless of whether the home is faith based and what the stance of that faith community may be. The use of pornography by the older generations may not be as extensive as that of the younger ones, but it is certainly happening. The internet offers something for everyone in the variety of pornographic videos available. These offerings are expanding daily so that anything we might say to characterize the menu today will have been surpassed by the time this is read.

Jennifer Hillman has suggested that there are both benefits and harms for older adults in the use of online pornography. She imagines someone who is wheelchair-bound or even bedridden now being able to access sexually stimulating materials that would be otherwise unavailable. The internet avoids the embarrassment of having to go to a public store and purchase the material. Since much of it is free, it fits the limited budgets of many retirees: "For older adults without a partner, with a partner who is unable to engage in sexual activity, or for older adults who want to incorporate the viewing of pornography into their sexual activity, online erotica and pornography can provide helpful fantasies and releases." However, the downside for older adults with more time for viewing is a susceptibility to addiction, which can interfere with normal sex life as one begins to think that the distorted, make-believe sexual world of pornography is the real world of sexual activity.[7] From her clinical perspective, Hillman can speak of helpful fantasies, but she also realizes that pornography represents potentially dangerous fantasies that objectify persons, not authentic depictions of truly loving sexual engagement.

A thorough discussion of the pornography phenomenon, the wide variety of its offerings, the debates about obscenity, the debates among feminist thinkers, the appalling use of illegal child pornography, and the attitudes of those who work in the industry is an enormous undertaking that is beyond the scope of our immediate concerns. Rather, our challenge is what we can say about the use of pornography from the standpoint of Christian faith. The sample church statements quoted above are clear indictments of pornography. They state the case against it in language that emphasizes its violation of all that is entailed in the truly loving blend of eros and agape that is at the heart of our commitment to justice in love—in both our personal and social relations.

I have sought to affirm the sexuality of later life as seen through the lens of Christian faith active in love. A first step was to show evidence that stereotypes of asexual older age were false. It turns out that one mark of the ongoing interest in sexual expression is the use of pornography. This is an ambiguous finding; it supports the premise that sexual interest remains alive and well in older years, but it also points to an unhealthy aspect of it. So having voiced our disapproval of pornography from the standpoint of Christian ethics, reflected in the positions of the churches, what shall we say about its use by some seniors?

I do not think we can lump all users into one category of "sinners." There are surely those who relish pornography and make a regular habit of using it. There are others who yield to the temptation to use it from time to time and end up feeling bad about it afterward. Those who struggle with their conscience in this way experience some of the spiritual damage pornography can inflict. There is grace for that struggle. Maybe some are alone and lonely, with desires but no prospects of relationship—perhaps suffering the disabilities of old age and desperate for some semblance of sexual experience. There is a sadness about that scenario, one that evokes not condemnation but compassion.

We have to live with the presence of the gigantic pornography industry for the foreseeable future. While we reject what pornography stands for, the best defense is the ongoing support of healthy, loving sexual relationships throughout the life cycle in witness to what is possible by grace.

NOTES

PREFACE

1 Evangelical Lutheran Church in America, *Journey Together Faithfully: The Church and Homosexuality* (Chicago: Evangelical Lutheran Church in America, 2003), https://tinyurl.com/yx9gqx5w.

2 Evangelical Lutheran Church in America, *Human Sexuality: Gift and Trust* (Chicago: Evangelical Lutheran Church in America, 2009).

3 James M. Childs Jr., "Eschatology, Anthropology, and Sexuality: Helmut Thielicke and the Orders of Creation Revisited," *Journal of the Society of Christian Ethics* 30, no. 1 (Spring/Summer 2010): 3–20.

4 James M. Childs Jr., "Aging and Sexuality," *Dialog: A Journal of Theology* 58, no. 4 (December 2019): 269–76.

CHAPTER ONE: ATTITUDES TOWARD AGING AND SEXUALITY

1 "IYOP at a Glance," International Year of Older Persons 1999, United Nations Department of Economic and Social Affairs Ageing, accessed December 16, 2020, https://tinyurl.com/y7hpueqy.

2 Statement by United Nations Secretary-General Kofi Annan, October 1, 1998, qtd. in "IYOP at a Glance."

3 Jacqui Smith, "The Fourth Age: A Period of Psychological Mortality," Max Planck Institute for Demographic Research, 2000, https://tinyurl.com/yybuerto. Stephen F. Barnes also notes, "Starting at about age 80 or 85, the Fourth Age includes the last years of adulthood. . . . The Third Age, spanning the postemployment years of 65 to 80 years . . . includes many positive aspects to aging in terms of relative good health and social engagement." Barnes, "Fourth Age—the Final Years of Adulthood," San Diego State University Interwork Institute, 2011, https://tinyurl.com/y6xm4gcc.

4 Jeanette C. Takamura, "The Future Is Aging," *Social Thought* 20, nos. 3–4 (September 2001): 9–10.

5 Takamura, 6. The myths she lists are taken from J. W. Rowe and R. L. Kahn, *Successful Aging* (New York: Pantheon, 1998).
6 Robert Youdin, *Psychology of Aging 101* (New York: Springer, 2016), 31–32.
7 Keith C. Meador and Shaun C. Henson, "Growing Old in a Therapeutic Culture," in *Growing Old in Christ*, ed. Stanley Hauerwas, Carol Bailey Stoneking, Keith C. Meador, and David Cloutier (Grand Rapids, MI: Eerdmans, 2003), 96–97.
8 Leni Marshall, "Thinking Differently about Aging: Changing Attitudes through the Humanities," *Gerontologist* 55, no. 4 (August 2015): 519–25.
9 Thomas M. Hess, "Attitudes toward Aging and Their Effects on Behavior," in *Handbook of Psychology of Aging*, 6th ed., ed. K. Warner Schaie, Ronald Abeles, and Timothy A. Salthouse (Cambridge, MA: Academic Press, 2006), 398–99.
10 Frits de Lange, *Loving Later Life: An Ethics of Aging* (Grand Rapids, MI: Eerdmans, 2015), 62–63. De Lange's chapter "Why We Do Not Love the Elderly" develops the theme of the traditional aversion to the aged and to aging, including a quote from a recent undergraduate student: "Old people make me feel sick" (65).
11 Merryn Gott, *Sexuality, Health, and Aging* (Maidenhead, Berkshire, England: Open University Press, 2005), 20.
12 Gott, 21.
13 Michael Bauer, Linda McAuliffe, and Deirdre Fetherstonhaugh, "Older People and Sexuality in Residential Aged Care: Reconstructing Normality," in *Ageing and Sexualities: Interdisciplinary Perspectives*, ed. Elizabeth Peel and Rosie Harding (London: Routledge, 2016), 120.
14 Eddie Cantor, Harry Warren, Dubin, and Jorg, "Keep Young and Beautiful," 1933, *Vocal Popular Sheet Music Collection*, score 2923, https://tinyurl.com/y398mo33.
15 Gott, *Sexuality*, 18.
16 Ron Long, "Becoming the Men We're Ceasing to Be: A Gay Agenda for Aging in a Youth Culture," *Theology and Sexuality* 2001, no. 15 (2001): 104.
17 Long, 102.
18 Long, 108.
19 Long, 112.
20 Jennifer Hillman, *Sexuality and Aging: Clinical Perspectives* (New York: Springer, 2012), 66.
21 Maggie L. Syme and Tracy J. Cohn, "Examining Aging Sexual Stigma Attitude among Adults by Gender, Age, and Generational Status," *Aging and Mental Health* 20, no. 1 (2016): 37, https://www.ncbi.nlm.nih.gov/pmc/articles/PMC4805428.
22 See the discussion of this history in Margaret Farley, *Just Love: A Framework for Christian Social Ethics* (New York: Continuum, 2008), 39–49.
23 Adrian Thatcher, *Thinking about Sex* (Minneapolis: Fortress Press, 2015), 20.

24 Karen A. McClintock, *Sexual Shame: An Urgent Need for Healing* (Minneapolis: Fortress Press, 2001).
25 Thatcher, *Thinking about Sex*, 21.
26 McClintock, *Sexual Shame*, 23.
27 McClintock, 24.
28 Arthur Krystal, "Old News: Why Can't We Tell the Truth about Aging?," *New Yorker*, November 4, 2019, 77.
29 Sylvan Tomkins, *Affect Imagery Consciousness*, vol. 2, *The Negative Affects* (New York: Springer, 1963), 201, qtd. in Virginia Burrus, *Saving Shame: Martyrs, Saints, and Other Abject Subjects* (Philadelphia: University of Pennsylvania Press, 2008), 46.
30 Gott, *Sexuality*, 21.
31 Gott, 21.
32 Studs Terkel, *Coming of Age: The Story of Our Century and Those Who Lived It* (New York: New Press, 1995).
33 Terkel, 1–5.
34 Terkel, 54.
35 Terkel, 231.
36 Terkel, 423–28.
37 Terkel, 427.
38 Terkel, 429.
39 Martin Luther, *The Babylonian Captivity of the Church*, in *Luther's Works*, vol. 36, ed. and trans. Abdel Ross Wentz (Philadelphia: Fortress Press, 1959), 113.
40 Evangelical Lutheran Church in America, *Evangelical Lutheran Worship* (Minneapolis: Augsburg Fortress, 2006), 227–37 (emphasis mine).
41 Randi S. Chance, "To Love and Be Loved: Sexuality and People with Physical Disabilities," *Journal of Psychology and Theology* 36, no. 3 (2002): 195–208.

Chapter Two: Sexuality in Older Age

1 Davide Zordan, "Too Old for That Kind of Thing? Sexuality and Unshakeable Desire in Dresen's *Cloud 9*," *Theology and Sexuality* 15, no. 3 (September 2009): 288.
2 Zordan, 289–90 (emphasis mine).
3 Zordan, 289.
4 J. Hillman, *Clinical Perspectives on Elderly Sexuality* (Dordrecht: Kluwer, 2000), 5–6, qtd. in Gott, *Sexuality*, 12.
5 Maggie L. Syme, "The Evolving Concept of Older Adult Sexual Behavior and Its Benefits," *Journal of the American Society on Aging* 38, no. 1 (Spring 2014): 37.

6 Farley, *Just Love*, 159.
7 Dena Bunis, "Two-Thirds of Older Adults Are Interested in Sex, Poll Says," *AARP*, May 3, 2019, https://tinyurl.com/y6dq3rdg.
8 Jennifer Hillman, "A Call for an Integrated Biopsychosocial Model to Address Fundamental Disconnects in an Emergent Field; Introduction to the Special Issue on 'Sexuality and Aging,'" *Ageing International* 36, no. 303 (2011), https://tinyurl.com/y3knx7w3.
9 Gott, *Sexuality*, 24–25.
10 Gott, 25–27.
11 Gott, 28–29.
12 Gott, 30–32.
13 Gott, 32–34.
14 Gott, 30.
15 Youdin, *Psychology of Aging*, 110.
16 Youdin, 111.
17 Youdin, 112.
18 Youdin, 111.
19 Youdin, 115.
20 Erin Dufault-Hunter, "The Downside of Getting It Up: How Viagra Reveals the Persistence of Patriarchy and the Need for Sexual Character," *Journal of the Society of Christian Ethics* 32, no. 1 (2012): 57–74.
21 Youdin, *Psychology of Aging*, 113.
22 Hillman, *Sexuality and Aging*, 257–58.
23 Hillman, 234–35.
24 Jane Traies, "Becoming Visible: De-marginalizing Older Lesbians in LGBT Ageing Discourse," in *Ageing and Sexualities: Interdisciplinary Perspectives*, ed. Elizabeth Peel and Rosie Harding (London: Routledge, 2016), 79–80, 91–92.
25 Hillman, *Sexuality and Aging*, 235–36.
26 Catherine Barret et al., "Social Connection, Relationships and Older Lesbian and Gay People," *Sexual and Relationship Therapy* 30, no. 1 (2015): 131–42, https://tinyurl.com/y39dyh94. This Australian study provides some helpful insights into this discussion.
27 Connie Goldman, *Late Life Love: Romance and New Relationships in Later Years* (Minneapolis: Fairview Press, 2006), 2.
28 Goldman, 38–39.
29 Goldman, 24–25.
30 Goldman, 46–47.
31 Goldman, 111.

Chapter Three: Living Options among Older Adults

1 Renee Stepler, "Number of U.S. Adults Cohabiting with a Partner Continues to Rise, Especially among Those 50 and Older," Pew Research Center, April 6, 2017, https://tinyurl.com/y6hrk67u.

2 Susan L. Brown and Matthew R. Wright, "Marriage, Cohabitation, and Divorce in Later Life," *Innovation in Aging* 1, no. 2 (September 2017), https://tinyurl.com/yxtppmcn.

3 Brown and Wright.

4 Susan L. Brown, Jennifer Roebuck Bulanda, and Gary R. Lee, "Transitions into and out of Cohabitation in Later Life," *Journal of Marriage and Family* 74, no. 4 (August 2012): 774–93, https://tinyurl.com/ydcbhugl.

5 Brown and Wright, "Marriage."

6 Brown and Wright.

7 Susan L. Brown and Sayaka Kawamura, "Relationship Quality among Cohabiters and Marrieds in Older Adulthood," *Social Science Research* 39, no. 5 (2010): 777–86, https://tinyurl.com/y8rmqjzx.

8 Goldman, *Late Life Love*, 75–76.

9 Goldman, 188–91.

10 Goldman, 70.

11 Goldman, 143.

12 Goldman, 54–55.

13 Traies, "Becoming Visible," 86.

14 Traies, 86–87.

15 United States Conference of Catholic Bishops, *Marriage: Love and Life in the Divine Plan* (Washington, DC: USCCB, 2009), https://tinyurl.com/cjre9kl, 26.

16 David Matzko McCarthy, "Cohabitation and Marriage," in *Leaving and Coming Home: New Wineskins for Sexual Ethics*, ed. David Cloutier (Eugene, OR: Cascade, 2010), 139, qtd. in Julie Hanlon Rubio, "Family Ethics: Beyond Sex and Controversy," *Theological Studies* 74 (January 1, 2013): 14.

17 Todd A. Salzman and Michael G. Lawler, *The Sexual Person: Toward a Renewed Catholic Anthropology* (Washington, DC: Georgetown University Press, 2008), 211–13.

18 "On Biblical Sexuality and Public Policy," Southern Baptist Convention, June 1, 2009, https://tinyurl.com/ycxt4r6a.

19 Evan Lenow, "Cohabitation in the Church," *Baptist Press*, August 14, 2013, https://tinyurl.com/y6y85aes. The article was first published in the *Alabama Baptist*, an online journal.

20 "Cohabiting Senior Couples: Financial and Moral Considerations," Focus on the Family, accessed March 15, 2020, https://tinyurl.com/yyhw2a55.

21 Irma Fast Dueck, "Without Rings and without Strings: Engaging Cohabitation in the Church," *Vision: A Journal for Church and Theology* 19, no. 1 (Spring 2018): 71–75.

22 Dueck, 75–76.

23 Dueck, 76.

24 A. L. Bary, "Living Together without Marriage," Lutheran Church Missouri Synod, 1998, https://www.lcms.org/about/beliefs.

25 Robert W. Weise, "Marriage: The Divine and Blessed Walk of Life," *Concordia Journal* 40, no. 1 (Winter 2014): 49.

26 Evangelical Lutheran Church in America, *Human Sexuality*, 2 (adopted by Churchwide Assembly, August 19, 2009).

27 Evangelical Lutheran Church in America, 8–9.

28 Evangelical Lutheran Church in America, 15.

29 Evangelical Lutheran Church in America, 16.

30 Evangelical Lutheran Church in America, 33.

31 "Resolution A086, 797," Episcopal Church USA, Blue Book Reports, https://www.generalconvention.org/bluebook2018.

32 Archives of the Episcopal Church, https://tinyurl.com/ybzm8zjo.

33 "Christian Perspectives on Marriage and Family Today: Householding, 836," Episcopal Church USA, Blue Book Reports, https://www.generalconvention.org/bluebook2018.

34 Julianna Menasce Horowitz, Nikki Graf, and Gretchen Livingston, "Marriage and Cohabitation in the U.S.," Pew Research Center, November 6, 2019, https://tinyurl.com/y2vzz466.

35 Robin Givhan, "Redefining Beauty," *National Geographic*, February 2020, 100.

Chapter Four: Sexual Life in Long-Term Care Facilities

1 Ann Christine Frankowski and Leanne J. Clark, "Sexual Intimacy in Assisted Living: Residents' Perspectives and Experiences," *Sexuality Research and Social Policy Journal of NSRC* 6 (2009): 25–37, https://tinyurl.com/y8g867ml.

2 Michael Bauer, Emily Haesler, and Deirdre Fetherstonhaugh, "Let's Talk about Sex: Older People's Views on the Recognition of Sexuality and Sexual Health in the Health-Care Setting," *Health Expectations* 19, no. 6 (October 2015): 1240,

https://doi.org/10.1111/hex.12418. This study used research based in the United States, Europe, and Australia.

3 Steven H. Miles and Kara Parker, "Sexuality in the Nursing Home: Iatrogenic Loneliness," *Generations: Journal of the American Society on Aging* 23, no. 1 (Spring 1999): 36–43.

4 Miles and Parker, 36–43.

5 Bauer, Haesler, and Fetherstonhaugh, "Let's Talk about Sex," 1245.

6 Frankowski and Clark, "Sexual Intimacy."

7 Frankowski and Clark.

8 Frankowski and Clark.

9 *Sexual Expression Policy Development: A Guide for Long-Term Care Facilities & Assisted Living Programs*, Iowa Office of the State Long-Term Care Ombudsman, November 2016, https://tinyurl.com/y5kfyp6w.

10 See the Health Facilities Division of the Colorado Department of Public Health and Environment, revised September 2004, https://tinyurl.com/yymgoklx.

11 See the Board of Aging and Long-Term Care—Ombudsman Program for the State of Wisconsin, accessed March 30, 2020, https://tinyurl.com/yyqyf4px (emphasis mine).

12 Robin Dessel and Mildred Ramirez, *Policies and Procedures concerning Sexual Expression at the Hebrew Home at Riverdale*, last updated April 2013, https://tinyurl.com/y6xu84tr.

13 Jennifer Sisk, "Sexuality in Nursing Homes: Preserving Rights, Promoting Well-Being," *AgingWell*, accessed December 8, 2020, https://tinyurl.com/y4ajmkp4.

14 John Gingrich, "Senior Sexuality: Intimacy Policy at Brethren Hillcrest Homes," *Brethren Life & Thought* (Winter and Spring 2010): 38–42.

15 Gingrich, 42.

16 For a succinct overview of Jewish sexual ethics and the diversity of views within that tradition, see "Judaism and Sex: Questions and Answers," My Jewish Learning, https://tinyurl.com/y2t3sks3.

17 Charles Bourchard, "Sex and Senior Living: Ethical Questions for Catholic Housing and Long-Term Care," *HCEUSA* (Winter 2019): 15.

18 Bourchard, 15–17.

19 Bourchard, 18.

20 Available as appendix B in "Capacity for Sexual Consent in Dementia in Long-Term Care," Society for Post-acute and Long-Term Care Medicine, March 2016, https://tinyurl.com/yytpms3s.

21 Peter A. Lichtenberg, "Sexuality and Intimacy in Long-Term Care," *Occupational Therapy in Health Care* 28, no. 1 (2014): 42–50, https://tinyurl.com/yygjm69v.

22 Lichtenberg.

23 Jennifer Hillman, "Sexual Consent Capacity: Ethical Issues and Challenges in Long-Term Care," *Clinical Gerontology* 48, no. 1 (2017): 44–45. See also Bauer, McAuliffe, and Fetherstonhaugh, "Older People and Sexuality," 128–29.

24 Eran Metzger, "Ethics and Intimate Sexuality in Long-Term Care," *AMA Journal of Ethics* 19, no. 7 (July 2017): 640–48, https://tinyurl.com/yyhp4ezp.

25 Metzger.

26 Lichtenberg, "Sexuality and Intimacy."

27 Lichtenberg.

28 Hillman, *Sexuality and Aging*, 147.

29 Derrick Y. McDaniel, "Sex and Seniors—a New Reality for the Elderly," HuffPost, April 6, 2017, https://tinyurl.com/yyth9lp2.

30 Hillman, *Sexuality and Aging*, 149.

31 Hillman, 148–49; McDaniel, "Sex and Seniors."

32 Youdin, *Psychology and Aging*, 121–23.

33 Amber Hollibaugh, "Sex, Senior Living, and LGBTQ Elders: Willful Ignorance Is No Longer an Option," *Aging Today* 32, no. 4 (July–August 2011): 11–12.

34 Tim R. Johnston, *Welcoming LGBT Residents: A Practical Guide for Senior Living Staff* (London: Routledge, 2020), see chapters 1 and 2.

35 SAGE, *LGBTQ Aging: The Case for Inclusive Long-Term Care Communities*, 2020, https://tinyurl.com/ybd6cqh3.

36 SAGE.

37 Kimberly Wilson et al., "Support Needs of Lesbian, Gay, Bisexual, and Transgender Older Adults in the Health and Social Environment," *Counselling and Spirituality* 35, no. 1 (2016): 21. See also a discussion of efforts by the federal Department of Health and Human Services, along with some state initiatives, to grant religious exemptions from present law to religiously affiliated nonprofit organizations receiving federal funds, allowing them to refuse services on the basis of religious conviction or "conscience." Some religiously affiliated long-term care facilities might then conceivably refuse services to LGBTQ folk, unmarried couples, and so on. Movement Advancement Project, Public Rights / Private Conscience Project, and SAGE, *Dignity Denied*, December 2017, https://tinyurl.com/y3z4ulp3.

38 Wilson et al.

Chapter Five: Sexuality, Values, and Vocation

1 My own work in this regard was published in *Christian Anthropology and Ethics* (Philadelphia: Fortress Press, 1978), 85–86.

2 Farley, *Just Love*, 116–17.

3 David M. Carr, *The Erotic Word: Sexuality, Spirituality, and the Bible* (New York: Oxford University Press, 2003), 143–44.

4 Carr, 147.

5 Carr, 149.

6 In this section, I will be drawing heavily on an article I previously published, "Eschatology, Anthropology, and Sexuality."

7 Leviticus 18:22 and 20:13; Romans 1:26–27; 1 Corinthians 6:9–11; and 1 Timothy 1:9–10 are the texts most cited. Appeals are also made to Genesis 19:1–11 (Sodom) and Judges 19:16–30 (Gibea), though even some conservative scholars doubt their relevance on the matter of same-gender sexual activity.

8 William Stacy Johnson, in his helpful book *A Time to Embrace: Same-Gender Relationships in Religion, Law, and Politics* (Grand Rapids, MI: Eerdmans, 2006), underscores the historical importance of the argument from orders of creation, noting that its positive claim for the institution of marriage links up with the negative argument from Scripture that prohibits all sexual activity outside of marriage, including gay and lesbian sex (46).

9 Paul Althaus, *The Ethics of Martin Luther*, trans. Robert C. Schultz (Philadelphia: Fortress Press, 1972), 85.

10 Martin Luther, *The Large Catechism*, in *The Book of Concord: The Confessions of the Evangelical Lutheran Church*, ed. Robert Kolb and Timothy J. Wengert (Minneapolis: Fortress Press, 2000), 414.

11 Max L. Stackhouse, "The Heterosexual Norm," in *Homosexuality and Christian Community*, ed. Choon-Leong Seow (Louisville, KY: Westminster John Knox, 1996), 136.

12 Robert A. J. Gagnon, *The Bible and Homosexual Practice: Texts and Hermeneutics* (Nashville: Abingdon Press, 2001), 62.

13 Helmut Thielicke, *Theological Ethics*, vol. 1, ed. William H. Lazareth (Philadelphia: Fortress Press, 1966), 439–40.

14 Helmut Thielicke, *The Ethics of Sex*, trans. John W. Doberstein (New York: Harper & Row, 1964), 105.

15 Thielicke, 103.

16 Thielicke, 283–88. Although he does not invoke the matter of procreation specifically in this discussion of homosexuality, the order of creation, which it stands at odds with, does include procreation as an element that is not absolute in practice but clearly a part of God's design (251–55).

17 Christian Batalden Scharen, *Marriage in the Sight of God: Theology, Ethics, and Church Debates over Homosexuality* (New York: University Press of America, 2000), 144–47.
18 Dietrich Bonhoeffer, *Creation and Fall: A Theological Exposition of Genesis 1–3*, English ed., ed. John W. de Gruchy, trans. Douglas Stephen Bax (Minneapolis: Fortress Press, 1997), 62.
19 Their work has been an important resource for the theological foundations of my argument, though I hasten to add that neither Pannenberg nor probably Moltmann would share my conclusions, let alone Bonhoeffer.
20 Wolfhart Pannenberg, *Jesus—God and Man*, trans. Lewis L. Wilkins and Duane A. Priebe (Philadelphia: Westminster Press, 1968), 66–69.
21 Wolfhart Pannenberg, *Systematic Theology*, vol. 2, trans. Geoffrey W. Bromiley (Grand Rapids, MI: Eerdmans, 1994), 163.
22 Jürgen Moltmann, *The Coming of God: Christian Eschatology*, trans. Margaret Kohl (Minneapolis: Fortress Press, 1996), 262–65.
23 Ted Peters, *God—the World's Future: Systematic Theology for a New Era* (Minneapolis: Fortress Press, 2000), 129.
24 Terrence E. Fretheim, *God and World in the Old Testament: A Relational Theology of Creation* (Nashville: Abingdon Press, 2005), 5–9.
25 Fretheim, 9.
26 Gustaf Wingren, *Man and the Incarnation*, trans. Ross Mackenzie (Philadelphia: Fortress Press, 1959), 32.
27 Stanley Grenz, *The Social God and the Relational Self* (Louisville, KY: Westminster John Knox, 2001), 303.
28 Miroslav Volf, *After Our Likeness: The Church as the Image of God* (Grand Rapids, MI: Eerdmans, 1998), 173.
29 I have spoken of these values of the kingdom of God as a revelation of the good toward which we strive in love in almost all my writings, including pertinent biblical references. See, for example, my *Ethics in the Community of Promise: Faith, Formation, and Decision*, 2nd ed. (Minneapolis: Fortress Press, 2006), 17–21.
30 Childs, 25–27.
31 James M. Childs Jr., *Ethics in Business: Faith at Work* (Minneapolis: Fortress Press, 1995), 51.
32 Evangelical Lutheran Church in America, *Human Sexuality*, 2.
33 Evangelical Lutheran Church in America, 8–9.

Chapter Six: Aging, Sexuality, and the Ethics of Christian Love

1 Childs, *Ethics in the Community*, 38. I will be using the basic concepts of that book throughout this chapter but developing their application in terms of the concerns of this book.

2 Farley, *Just Love*, 231.

3 Robert A. Guelich, *The Sermon on the Mount* (Waco, TX: Word, 1982), 67.

4 Gustavo Gutiérrez, *A Theology of Liberation*, trans. and ed. Caridad Inda and John Eagelson (Maryknoll, NY: Orbis, 1973), 297.

5 De Lange, *Loving Later Life*, 29.

6 De Lange, 29–39.

7 De Lange, 81.

8 De Lange, 39.

9 De Lange, 96.

10 Childs, *Ethics in the Community*, 40.

11 Paul Tillich, *Systematic Theology*, vol. 3 (Chicago: University of Chicago Press, 1963), 138.

12 "Majority of Americans Now Believe in Cohabitation," Barna, June 24, 2016, https://tinyurl.com/mfe89m5. Though slightly different from the Pew poll cited earlier, the results compare well.

Appendix

1 "What Does the Bible Say about Masturbation?," Christian Bible Reference, accessed April 25, 2020, https://tinyurl.com/rkewbpt.

2 Office of the General Assembly Presbyterian Church (USA), *Presbyterians and Human Sexuality 1991* (Louisville, KY: Office of the General Assembly Presbyterian Church [USA], 1991), https://tinyurl.com/y8cvj4qk.

3 Catholic Education Resource Center, accessed April 25, 2020, https://tinyurl.com/y29ns3at.

4 Farley, *Just Love*, 235. See also the discussion in Salzman and Lawler, *Sexual Person*, 153–56.

5 Book of Discipline of the United Methodist Church, 2016, https://tinyurl.com/y5ee377m.

6 Evangelical Lutheran Church in America, *Message on . . . Commercial Sexual Exploitation* (Chicago: Department for Studies of the Division for Church in Society, 2001), 14–15, https://tinyurl.com/y4juudlj.

7 Hillman, *Sexuality and Aging*, 260.

INDEX